The 7 Kata

Toyota Kata, TWI, and Lean Training

CONRAD SOLTERO
PATRICE BOUTIER

 **CRC Press**
Taylor & Francis Group
Boca Raton London New York

CRC Press is an imprint of the
Taylor & Francis Group, an **informa** business

A PRODUCTIVITY PRESS BOOK

CRC Press
Taylor & Francis Group
6000 Broken Sound Parkway NW, Suite 300
Boca Raton, FL 33487-2742

© 2012 by Taylor & Francis Group, LLC
CRC Press is an imprint of Taylor & Francis Group, an Informa business

No claim to original U.S. Government works

Printed in the United States of America on acid-free paper
Version Date: 20120501

International Standard Book Number: 978-1-4398-8077-7 (Paperback)

Visit the Taylor & Francis Web site at
http://www.taylorandfrancis.com

and the CRC Press Web site at
http://www.crcpress.com

Contents

Foreword

Conrad Soltero and Patrice Boutier are two of the earliest and most consistently diligent students, practitioners, and teachers of the TWI methods. Through their hard work and steadfastness they have made a major contribution to the resurgence of TWI in the United States. Their experience with TWI over the past ten years clearly shows in this work—most notably in how they are able to adroitly place TWI into the larger realm of Lean practice and what the world has learned about Lean since the TWI programs were first developed in the 1940s.

By looking at the TWI methods, JI/JM/JR and JS, as everyday practices that become as much a part of "who we are" than simply "what we do," they show the continuing power of these methods to alter ourselves and improve our daily work. Although each of the TWI methodologies can stand on its own, through their integrated view of these methods as *kata* or *human practice*, Soltero and Boutier show how the methods complement each other, as well as the later Lean approaches, and provide a holistic approach to frontline leadership. It is in this well-rounded approach to skills development that we begin to perceive, as the authors clearly show, an image of a learning organization that can tap into its true human potential.

Patrick Graupp
TWI Institute Senior Master Trainer
Author of *The TWI Workbook: Essential Skills for Supervisors Implementing TWI: Creating and Managing a Skills-Based Culture* and *Getting to Standard Work in Health Care: Using TWI to Create a Foundation for Quality Care*

Foreword

Mike Rother tackles two overarching questions in his book *Toyota Kata*. One has to do with the unseen routines and thinking that lie behind Toyota's success. The other has to do with how other companies can develop similar routines and thinking in their organizations.[*] By answering these questions Rother has opened the door for other organizations to reach new levels of performance in human endeavor by adopting the Improvement and Coaching Kata to create more effective ways of working, and of working together in an organization.

The Improvement Kata is defined by Rother as being a set of behavioral guidelines that managers and leaders at Toyota teach people by guiding them in making real improvements in real processes as part of how people are managed day to day. The *Learn by Doing* technique is easily recognized as emanating from TWI. We also learned from Liker and Meier (2007) in *Toyota Talent* that TWI Job Instruction (JI) is deeply integrated into the overall Toyota Production System. This raises a question about the roles JI and other TWI programs have when managers and leaders teach people at Toyota when guiding them in making real improvements in the workplace.

Influenced by Mike Rother's book, Conrad Soltero and Patrice Boutier wrote *The 7 Kata: Toyota Kata, TWI, and Lean Training* to show how the basic skill sets that TWI and the Toyota Kata teach can boost an organization's Lean transformation. Perhaps we can better appreciate the challenge taken on by these authors by examining how Toyota rolled out the learning points from the "Ohno line." By 1950 Ohno's thoughts on kaizen, flow, multi-process handling, visual control, and standardized work, etc. were established in his mind, and coached to his disciples who spread these learning points to other areas in the company.[†]

---

[*] Mike Rother, *Toyota Kata*, Rother & Company, LLC, 2010, Foreword.
[†] Art Smalley, *Summary of Interview with Mr. Isao Kato about TWI Influence on TPS & Kaizen*, February 8, 2006, www.ArtofLean.com

TWI came into the picture in 1950 when the company was near bankruptcy when Toyota management responded to a request from the labor union to create some form of supervisor development and training. It was also in 1950 that Taiichi Ohno was completing experiments that he started in 1945 to improve flow and to create a more efficient production system in his line. According to Isao Kato, Ohno's thoughts about kaizen, flow, multi-process handling, visual control, and standardizing work were established in his head, and his disciples were being coached in the methods when TWI was being introduced to Toyota. After reviewing their options, Toyota adopted TWI because it was an existing program that had received favorable reviews since being introduced to Japan by the U.S. Occupational Government after WWII. First Job Instruction (JI) was reintroduced in 1951, then in succession Job Methods (JM) in 1952 and, and Job Relations (JR) in 1953.

"In a historical sense JI came at a critical juncture for Toyota as Mr. Ohno was now in a position between 1950 and 1955 to begin to roll out the learning points from the 'Ohno line' to other areas of the company. . . . For this reason I *(Mr. Kato)* believe and I think that Mr. Ohno would agree that JI had by far the biggest impact on TPS formulation." Mr. Kato ended this interview with advice for companies implementing Lean. "If people want to succeed with lean or TPS they have to emphasize people development and making leaders capable of delivering improvement. TWI is a great starting point, even today, and a hidden strength of Toyota's production system."[*]

As experienced TWI trainers with 15 years of combined experience teaching TWI as part of a Lean strategy, Soltero and Boutier provide insight into how the Seven Kata, which include TWI programs of Job Instruction (JI), Job Methods (JM), Job Relations (JR), Job Safety (JS) and Problem Solving (PS), can be used as a starting point for continual improvements. Their breakthrough effort to explain the bond between TWI and Toyota Kata and to make this connection known within the Lean community will no doubt open the door for other TWI and Kata practitioners to discover other behavioral guidelines and practices that may still be hidden in the open at Toyota. They point out that the practical routines of these Seven Kata, when practiced repeatedly, provide the skills that a modern workforce needs to react to change and to strive toward continuous improvement. This

---

[*] Art Smalley, *Summary of Interview with Mr. Isao Kato about TWI Influence on TPS & Kaizen,* February 8, 2006, www.ArtofLean.com

book makes known in practical ways that the "respect for people" core of Toyota continues to be a discipline that distinguishes best those companies that will continue to adapt and grow.

Robert J. Wrona
Executive Director
TWI Institute

Foreword

In the late 1980s I began my Lean journey, actually quite unknowingly. I was hired as a manufacturing engineer by Aisin Seiki, a Toyota Group Company. They were in the process of transplanting to North America to supply Toyota's operations, which, at that time, were in Cambridge, Ontario (TMMC), Fremont, California (NUMMI), and the start-up operation in Georgetown, Kentucky (TMMK). The operation for which I would be responsible—brake manufacturing—was not yet built. I took the position, not because it was a Toyota Group Company or because of the opportunity to learn Toyota Production System (TPS), but because it was a plant start up involving machining and assembly. I knew nothing of the TPS, nor was I overly interested or uninterested when it was discussed or when I received TPS training during my lengthy training in Japan. TPS seemed to make sense to me, so it was fine.

Fast forward a few years when I left Aisin and took a new position with a company that hired me because of my experience in machining and assembly, as well as in TPS. The second day in my new position I realized that *the rest of the industrial world did not function like the company I had just left* (Aisin and Toyota). By the way, they had also hired me because I was *supposed* to know something about TPS. That was a very enlightening moment because of the long-term impact it had on my career and life. At that same moment, I realized, "Oh my! I had better know something about this TPS thing!"

My actual TPS development really began at that point. I did have the actual experience of the methods, machines, lines, Japanese engineers, discussions, daily work improvements, standard work development, etc. to reflect on deeply as I worked on TPS in my new position. That tangible, hands-on experience, although I was not thinking about it much while working for Aisin, proved invaluable as I knew *what was possible*. In the long run, I believed it helped me even more, as I would have to do much in-depth reflection and many deep discussions with my colleagues to understand and figure out all of the *whats*, *whys*, and *hows* of the work we were doing. I spent many years in this sandbox, learning valuable, and often difficult, lessons of TPS and its role in manufacturing and business. We had many successes and many failures. The learning, in hindsight, was astonishing.

I was very conscious of the one lesson that eluded me—the success of (or more aptly put, unsuccessful) implementation of standard work for the operators with whom I worked. The lines, machines, fixtures, material handling, and even standard work documents and development were done very well, even upon reflection of my experience over the 15 to 20 years since I did this work. I knew, even then, "something" was missing, but I did not know what that "something" was. And that frustrated me.

Fast forward several years. I had two books on my desk to read that would also soon significantly impact my career and life. The first one I read was *Becoming Lean* edited by Jeff Liker (2007), and the second was *Gemba Kaizen* (1997) by Masaaki Imai. In *Becoming Lean*, in the chapter by John Shook, he briefly mentions a World War II program called Training Within Industry (TWI). And I thought, "What the heck does some WWII program have to do with the Toyota Production System?" It was interesting, but I continued reading without giving it much more thought until the next month, while reading *Gemba Kaizen*, Imai discusses TWI even further. I realized I had to find out what the heck this program had to do with the Toyota Production System! What I found out changed my view of production and answered my question regarding my lingering feeling that *something* was missing.

TWI was the missing piece of the puzzle. It was much more than a training program, a tool, or the elements of kaizen and standard work. It was one of the foundational underpinnings—or *kata*—to the success of the Toyota Production System. In fact, it is a building block to the Toyota Way. I came to realize that the kata embedded in TWI was so much more than the foundation upon which Standard Work was built. It was integral to the success of the entire organizational structure, thinking and behavior.

Mike Rother's groundbreaking book, *Toyota Kata*, discloses the functional behavior patterns that helped make the Toyota Way a success, and also creates the context in which TPS is frequently referenced as the *Thinking Production System*. The behavior pattern leads to the thinking pattern. After *Toyota Kata* was published I told Mike that he succinctly and accurately explained something I had learned intuitively over my years experiencing the practice and development of TPS—learn by doing—but never had the ability to explain to others until *Toyota Kata*.

Now with *The 7 Kata*, Patrice Boutier and Conrad Soltero dive in and explain in detail the intimate and critical relationship between Toyota Kata and TWI. This is a critical understanding that organizations *must* realize to be successful at both, because they are essentially the same source. *The 7 Kata* explains the DNA of these indispensable skills (behaviors) and analysis (thinking) that organizations have been struggling with for nearly thirty years—to unleash the power behind actuating their entire workforce at all levels to make improvements everyday across the entire organizational structure.

Jim Huntzinger
President/Founder
Lean Frontiers

Preface

Globalization is pitting lower-wage countries against their higher-wage counterparts. Increasing access to education in the BRIC (Brazil, Russia, India, and China) countries is taking market share away from the United States while simultaneously creating new market opportunities, and this trend doesn't seem to be letting up. All things being equal, the greatest competitive advantage that any 21st century organization can expect will come through synergisms created by employees skilled not only in their area of educated specialty, but also in enhancing organizational dynamics.

Optimized organizational dynamics can now be trained to the workforce through standardized training methods and repeated practice. For example, America's community and junior colleges have been successful in teaching the trades because skills learned and practiced while in school are applied immediately after the training, on the job. The same has not been true for softer management and supervisory skills. This "trade school" methodology can now be replicated when teaching the organizational skills that can ultimately make the competitive difference.

We mean to show how the basic skill sets that Training Within Industry (TWI) and the Toyota Kata teach can boost an organization's Lean transformation. Globalism is making management's organizational skills a competitive differentiator, and we believe that daily practice of the Seven Kata provides a discernible path toward those ends.

Through the National Institute of Standards and Technology's Manufacturing Extension Partnership (NIST MEP) and the Texas Manufacturing Assistance Center (TMAC), we both have had the opportunity to come to understand innovation through our access to many of America's recognized luminaries of innovation. As such, we believe the connection of disparate concepts and the resulting synergisms are what drive innovation, for no single innovation ever occurred in a vacuum. All arise because of some useful synergistic effect that is a combination of previous knowledge. We also readily admit that many organizations throughout the world have captured "the magic" of synergism, Toyota being a flamboyant example.

As with all newly realized interpretations of technology, we stand on the shoulders of those who blazed trails before us. Johann Friedrich Herbart and Charles R. Alan are ancestors of the modern industrial kata. Channing Dooley and the four horsemen of the World War II–era Training Within Industry (TWI) Service, and also Toyoda, Ohno, and even Shigeo Shingo, should be considered the forefathers of the Seven Kata. Patrick Graupp and Bob Wrona of the TWI Institute, as well as Mike Rother, are the figurative parents of the Seven Kata. We are fortunate to be able to stand on the shoulders of Bob, Patrick, and Mike in our interpretation and repackaging of this age-old base of knowledge. For this, we are grateful.

We whole-heartedly believe that we stood in the right place at the right time with the right information and now have the opportunity to begin the process of transforming the way America works. This is granted to us through our rare position as players in American industrial extension.

Shigeo Shingo's contribution to Toyota is a prime example of what can be achieved when the captains of industry collaborate with industrial extension. As a consultant with the Japan Management Association (JMA), Shingo played an integral role in communicating—through standard training—how Toyota would develop its quality and management systems into a single entity.

American industrial extension is a consistent source of training and instruction of world-class practices that America's small businesses must have to outcompete both local and global rivals. The organizational and management technologies that can make a real difference in our global marketplace should not be accessible solely to those who can afford private consultants. This, like the raising of an army or the building of an interstate highway system, is a job that only government, at some level, can and must undertake. Industrial extension is one of the places where the economic development rubber meets the road.

Taiichi Ohno knew what he wanted and was able to access a standard method for delivering it to Toyota's employees and suppliers. Through the delivery of the JMA P-courses (production technology courses), Shingo became an impact player in the development of the Toyota Production System. Shingo was also the bridge for delivering these practices to Toyota's supply chain (small business).

Our only regret is that America's industrial extension services are limited to manufacturing. It is with our deepest conviction that we believe that management and organizational technologies like TWI, the Toyota Kata, and their offspring, the Seven Kata, should be readily available to all of America's industrial sectors. Of course, as consultants and trainers with long tenures in industrial extension, we are somewhat biased.

What This Book Is About

Back in the late 1980s and early 1990s, much of America was going through a period of concerns about Japan's growing economic strength. Many economists were calculating how many years it would be before the gross national product of Japan would be greater than America's. As a result, trade missions were deployed and many academics visited Japan to try to understand why this was so. As we now know, things changed and Japan turned out not to be the juggernaut that some thought it was. To not learn from Japan's post–World War II economic successes, however, would constitute neglect.

During that period, I faintly remember watching a news piece that attempted to explain some of Japan's advantages over the United States. Education and training were pointed to as underlying reasons. The statement that stood out and stuck in my mind was that even though the United States was superior in technological advancement and had a much deeper base of knowledge, we could not match the level of Japan's lowest common educational expectation for the average citizen. The report went on to explain that Japan's population had attained the highest average level of education in the world.

It would behoove our policymakers to understand that to compete in the 21st century workers must be skilled in the tenets of organizational dynamics, as well as be highly adaptable. When a person moves into the workforce, if he or she has not earned a college education, the probability of ever doing so drops precipitously with every year away from school. In the new economic order, some geographic regions will not be able to compete, at least not fast enough to bring economic relief or development. The answer to this quandary lies in accessibility to a robust vocational education system and the proliferation of the Seven Kata.

We detail how any organization in pursuit of operational excellence can most readily make advances toward that goal by adopting the way of kata. We devote a chapter to each of the Seven Kata and suggest possible courses of action dependent on an organization's particular strengths and constraints. We also advise the reader against mistakes that we have either experienced or witnessed during our years of assisting customers. Our goal is to provide the student of Lean with an awareness of where and how the seven skill sets apply on their Lean journey, without dictating a specific recipe.

The following is a quick preview of the key points covered in the individual chapters.

Chapter 1, Weapons for the Economic Warrior, explains how organizational skills are quickly becoming the price of admission just to compete in the 21st century's global economy. For far too long, much of the Lean community has blindly applied Lean's tools without regard to kaizen, wrongly assuming that the improvements brought about by the tools is kaizen. By introducing the Japanese cultural characteristics of syncretism and ritual and tying them to Lean's seemingly contradictory requirements of adaptability and standardization, this myth is dispelled. These requirements will be connected to the way of the kata. Hopefully, you will gain an ethereal sense that somehow Frederick Taylor met Siddhartha Gautama Buddha and Lean was born. The chapter concludes by reminding leaders of the importance of Lean knowledge and participation by leadership for any Lean journey.

Chapter 2, The Improvement Kata: Kaizen, opens by closely associating the Improvement Kata to kaizen. A clear distinction between improvement kaizen and maintenance kaizen is made, and the Improvement Kata is categorized as improvement kaizen. The chapter proceeds by introducing value stream analysis as the necessary aligning factor for Improvement Kata activities. The majority of the chapter focuses on the Improvement Kata steps and coaching points. *Yokoten* is introduced as a method for information sharing and how it should be considered as yet another factor in aligning Improvement Kata activities. The chapter culminates with a short discussion on kaizen events and Improvement Kata prioritization.

Chapter 3, The JI Nested Kata, begins by introducing a fictitious first day of work that closely resembles the personnel intake process of many organizations. The development of on-the-job (OJT) training is briefly discussed in order to demonstrate the chasm that exists between modern practices and known best practices that were developed almost 200 years ago. The inextricable link between OJT and standardization, a hallmark of Lean, is also explained.

The chapter then picks up with the multiple kata that are inherent in the JI Kata. It reviews each kata precisely and explains their synergistic support that becomes the framework for any type of OJT. In conclusion, the chapter details how to get started building a comprehensive OJT program.

Chapter 4, The Coaching Kata, starts by highlighting the connection of the JI Kata with coaching in general and the Coaching Kata specifically. The differences are defined between the development of coaches and higher-level Lean teachers we label "preceptors." Coaching philosophy and coaching are addressed briefly. Emphasis is placed on the importance of using the feedback from a coach based on experiences to evolve any specific kata. The revisions made to the Improvement Kata are explained as an example of this evolution. The chapter travels full circle by reverting to the TWI JI course's training timetable as an approach to tracking the development of kata coaches. Chapter 4 closes with the Coaching Kata's undeniable connection to the TWI JR foundations for good relations and points for coaching the PS Kata.

Chapter 5, The Problem Solving (PS) Kata, starts by admonishing those organizations that do not solve problems correctly. The chapter then reviews the details of the PS Kata. Other known Toyota problem solving methods are compared and contrasted to the PS Kata as well as to the TWI problem-solving methodology. The chapter ends by defining the role of Six Sigma in a problem-solving regime.

Chapter 6, The JR Kata: The Cultural Fortifier, identifies the JR Kata as a problem-solving tool focusing on relations. Since the Improvement Kata is identified as a cultural modifier, the JR Kata is assigned the role of fortifying the kata culture. A distinction is made between the Improvement Kata's modifying role in facilitating collaboration in comparison to the JR Kata's fortifying role in facilitating conciliation. The coaching and practice of the JR Kata are then treated followed by a brief explanation of how A3 thinking can be included with the JR Kata analysis.

Chapter 7, The JS Kata: The Duplex Kata, explains the dual nature of the JS Kata. Depending on how it is applied, it can be used for both improvement as well as problem-solving activities. The chapter also includes a discussion on the important connection between the JS Kata and the JI Key Point Kata. The chapter ends with a novel application of 5-Why analysis that is also related to the PS Kata.

Chapter 8, The JM Kata: Kipling's Kata, opens with a relevant rhyme by Rudyard Kipling. The chapter progresses by pointing to the JM Kata's ancient roots in scientific inquiry. The JM Kata is associated with improvement kaizen, the Improvement Kata, and even value stream analysis. The chapter also connects JM to kaizen *teian*, *nemawashi*, and A3 thinking.

Chapter 9, Submit to the Kata, is the conclusion of the book. It aims to appeal to the common sense of every leader by pointing to adaptability as essential to transformation, with the kata being "the key to adaptability." We end by explaining our discovery of the bond between TWI and the way of kata and our calling to make this connection known within the Lean community.

Acknowledgments

We are grateful to all the institutions and programs that have nurtured our professional and intellectual curiosities. These institutions and programs are ultimately made up of mentors, colleagues, and friends for whom acknowledgment of their personal support for our endeavors is in order.

Professionally, our immediate supervisors and colleagues have had the greatest influence on us. Without their collegiality, our tenure in industrial extension would have been cut short.

Intellectually, Bob Trachtenburg, Bob Wrona, and Mike Rother have each played a critical role in affording us access to Training Within Industry (TWI) and the Toyota Kata, the subject of this book. For the past decade, Patrick Graupp has been our TWI sensei and a truly inspiring role model for instruction and coaching. We thank him for sharing his knowledge and insights in a kind and friendly manner. Patrick has played the key role in repatriating TWI in a manner that is consistent with the intentions of its creators, members of America's greatest generation.

Through the Toyota Kata, Mike Rother has once and for all definitively bridged the training and application chasm with his application of deliberate practice to improvement and problem-solving efforts. The unification of TWI and deliberate practice became the obvious next step that we were fortunate enough to recognize, but only because of the efforts of the aforementioned. Mike's attitude of open discovery and encouragement on this project and to others to learn more about how to make change effective with everyone is unbelievable.

We are also privileged to have been able to work with our incredibly skilled graphic arts goddess, Amy Lyn Smith. We sincerely thank her for her patience and ability to keep us caught up. We also want to thank Joe "Blablazo" Lopez, who took time out of his busy schedule as a popular graphic novelist to consult with us on our desire for a simple yet highly symbolic book cover.

Finally, we would be remiss if we failed to mention our deep appreciation to our executive editor Michael Sinocchi, project coordinator Jessica Vakili, and project editor Robin Lloyd-Starkes. Their advice and support were instrumental in our ability to complete this work.

I (Pat) would like to extend thanks to the Texas Manufacturing Assistance Center (TMAC) and the University of Texas at Arlington. Specifically, I'd like to thank Don Liles and Drew Casani for providing a learning and working environment for me to assist Texas companies to better compete in a changing world. I also thank Mark Sessumes, who has been my mentor for six years and first suggested that I learn about TWI, and Frank Groenteman, who has always been willing to help me at any time and was instrumental in encouraging me to join TMAC. Without their encouragement along my TWI and Lean journey, this work would not have been possible. Working with Conrad on my first attempt at real writing has been a learning experience. His unceasing pursuit of excellence and his compassion and patience have been well worth the time and sharing.

I also want to thank my friends and coworkers, who have always encouraged me. My family has been super-supportive, allowing me space, time, and a very great deal of assistance. My parents, Jean and Genevieve, brought me up to cherish life and sacrificed to help launch my career. Without their major decision to move our family to the United States, my life would have been dramatically different. My eldest daughter Danielle and my two younger children Rachel and Andrew have all clearly understood the time and commitment needed to write this book. Then, of course, I'd like to thank my wonderful, charming wife, Bernadette. She has been most understanding and helpful in far too many ways to enumerate. Her editing assistance has been invaluable.

I (Conrad) need to recognize the role that many of my colleagues played in helping me conceptualize each of the chapters. My colleague in El Paso, Jesus Reverol, provided valuable input on the nexus between TWI Job Relations and the Improvement Kata. I was also able to formulate a working concept on the Job Safety Kata through our many hours of discussion on the matter. Jesus translated the entire Job Safety course into Spanish for the TWI Institute and was able to quickly identify and relate many of the concepts that I write about in Chapter 7.

I would also like to acknowledge my two mentors from TMAC Metroplex. Alberto Yanez mentored me many years ago when I began my industrial extension career. A seasoned consultant when I first met him, he taught me a lot. I am fortunate to still be able to keep in contact with him through our continuing work with TMAC. Even though Mark Sessumes and I have worked in different time zones for the past 14 or so years, we have had a continuous, ongoing conversation about all things Lean. Mark has been a tremendous intellectual asset in my understanding of Lean concepts. He is truly the type of colleague whom I hope everyone has an opportunity to associate with at least once in their career. Thanks, Mark!

Of course, my TWI colleague and coauthor, Patrice Boutier, should be acknowledged for putting up with me during this endeavor. He kept an eye on my blind spot and always challenged my assumptions. I initially thought he would be a good choice as my coauthor, and he has exceeded my expectations during this project.

When I first learned about the New York Technology Development Organization's (TDO) redevelopment of the TWI program back in 2002, my director, Stan Czacki, provided me the latitude I needed to obtain certification in each of the TWI courses. My current director, Hilario Gamez, and I worked together as colleagues for the better part of 10 years before he took over for Stan Czacki. Since then, he has maintained support of my professional goals. Hilario is not only one of the brightest individuals I'll ever know, he is also the most honest person I've ever met.

Many thanks to my two other colleagues in El Paso, Hector Lopez and Benito Flores, who always give me interesting content to ponder. Besides being a valued colleague, Hector is also a friend.

My parents have always been avid cheerleaders for me, which has always been reassuring. For that, I am grateful. My sister, Athena Marusich, is a small business owner and one of the types of people who keep America economically strong. I always keep her in mind when I work with small and closely held businesses. My brother, Jason, the insurance executive, keeps me briefed on what's hot in American big business and remains in my mind's eye when I deal with corporate types. My siblings are constant reminders of the breadth of American business.

Most of all, I must acknowledge my most cherished best friend of 30 years, Dana Gray. She has provided the calming environment that allows me to be more creative than I might otherwise be. I cannot forget about our kitty, Stalker, because she, too, is a very calming influence.

Chapter 1

Weapons for the Economic Warrior

1.1 Skills, Not Tools

Medieval swordsmen knew that their success in battle relied not only on how lethal their weapon was, but also how suitable their skill was. Toyota doesn't rely on brilliant people as their weapon of profitability; Toyota relies on average people and teaches them the skills most suitable to continuously improve.[1]

This book will provide the reader with the seven weapons necessary to outcompete economic rivals. These weapons, or skills, provide the workforce with the ability to adapt to changing conditions, a hallmark of Lean. Like the seven swords depicted on the cover of this book, the seven skills promoted will require their own specialized techniques and proper application. For almost 30 years, Lean has been the enigmatic golden ring that far too many organizations have reached for but have failed to grasp. We believe this is due to management's misapplication of some tools, and ignorance of the standard skills that all managers must practice daily.

Lean is not a set of tools to be implemented but rather a set of practiced skills that facilitate the modification of organizational culture. Our (Patrice Boutier's) definition of a Lean culture may be long, but it is encapsulating: "...one that capitalizes on the entire workforce's involvement in creative problem solving and continuous improvement, reaching beyond the competition by innovatively developing best practices." A Lean culture is based on

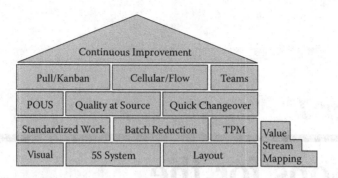

Figure 1.1 House of Lean.

the standardized thinking skills that a workforce possesses. Only then can Lean tools be more adroitly used. An explanation distinguishing the known tools of Lean with these standard skills for Lean is in order.

Figure 1.1 depicts the house of Lean that we in the National Institute of Standards and Technology's Manufacturing Extension Partnership (NIST MEP) have used for years in explaining Lean concepts. The building blocks of the house are some of the Lean tools that most practitioners, in one way or another, have advocated. To be certain, these tools are robust and work well. The "connective tissue" that joins these tools into a cohesive set of practices, however, has gone mostly unnoticed by the Lean community for far too long. Regardless of industry or process, the connective tissue referred to is dependent on the habits of mind that are practiced day in and day out by everyone. These habits of mind, good or bad, predicate the organization's productivity and ability to adapt and improve successfully.

1.2 Toyota's Connective Tissue

Arguments can be made asserting that Taiichi Ohno is the father of the Toyota Production System. Regardless, Ohno certainly played a critical role as a participant in the development of Toyota's strategic objectives. In a meeting between Eliyahu Goldratt and Taiichi Ohno that took place in Chicago in the late 1980s, Ohno admitted to doing his best to confuse American and European visitors to Toyota by focusing on tools, techniques, and the seven wastes while neglecting to fully inform on "his system."

Ohno stated that he was proud to be Japanese and wanted his country to succeed. He added that he believed that "his system" was a way he could help the nation become modern and industrialized and therefore had no problem sharing Toyota's insights with other Japanese companies, even Toyota's biggest competitors. He went on to say, "I was very, very concerned that you Americans and the Europeans would understand what we were doing, copy it, and defeat us in the marketplace."[2]

From these statements, it is obvious that Ohno was himself an economic warrior, an industrial samurai of sorts. In the 25 or so years since Goldratt and Ohno's meeting, most American and European Lean consultants have focused on the elimination of waste. Unfortunately, many of us have not been critical enough to realize that the elimination of waste is the product of the tools that Ohno was happy to share and some other ingredient that he purposely left for us to figure out.

One other telling aspect of Goldratt's meeting with Ohno that directly relates to what we will share in the coming chapters has to do with Ohno's method of improvement. When asked why his system worked, Ohno responded that he did not know, only that he kept trying different things, retained what worked, and discarded what didn't. As we will explain in the next chapter, a spirit of experimentation is all one needs to continually make improvements.[3]

The spirit of experimentation to be described is the connective tissue of Lean.

1.3 Skills of the Warrior

So what is this "connective tissue" or skill set that the workforce must possess? Recall that skills are different from knowledge. Knowledge, for example, is something you know and can get from seeing, listening, witnessing, or reading. Skill, on the other hand, is something that can only be attained through continued practice.[4] We cannot, therefore, merely inform the workforce on how to do something. It must actually be practiced repetitively for it to become a habit of mind. Not only do the Seven Kata define what skills an experienced manager working in a continual improvements environment must have, but they also provide the means for obtaining those skills.

Managers must be able to improve their processes in a practical and immediate way (Improvement Kata[5]). They must be able to pass on knowledge and skills to each other (Job Instruction Kata,[6] Coaching Kata[7]). They must have people skills to work together (Job Relations Kata[8]). They must be able to solve problems when problems arise (Problem-Solving Kata[9]). The need also exists to analyze and improve productivity, efficiency (Job Methods Kata[10]), and safety conditions (Job Safety Kata[11]). The one commonality between all seven of these skills is the requirement of repeated practice. The connective tissue previously mentioned comprises these seven skills, the skills of the economic warrior.

Whether the behaviors of the workforce are referred to as policies, standards, procedures, habits of mind, or second nature matters not. Kata are the proven way to instill desired behavior patterns into individuals.[12,13] We will explore the relationship between Japanese kata, American ingenuity, and world-class performance. We will then conclude this chapter with a bit of guidance on the suggested approach to this book.

As the word *kata* may be unfamiliar, a brief explanation is in order. A kata is commonly associated with Japanese martial arts. Specifically, it means form.[14] It is what one unfamiliar with martial arts might witness in a neighborhood karate studio: students organized in rows moving uniformly in demonstrating timed strikes (punches and kicks), blocks, and throws. The casual observer might assume that this is done so that the movements come more naturally during actual combat; that would only be partially correct. A kata is also a method for transferring knowledge from the master of a previous generation to students of a future generation.[15] This additional feature makes a kata more than just an exercise regimen. It is the conveyance mechanism for skills development as well as a time capsule for the future.

So, in a more minimalist way, the kata can be understood as the performance of a structured daily routine. Individuals who have had some level of involvement in martial arts have told us that a kata is a form, pattern, or type of practice. These descriptions convey much. A form relates contextual differences; there are many kata. A pattern is standardized. Practice indicates repetition. None of these descriptions, however, convey the significance of kata as the cultural modifier that they can be.

A kata is most parochially described by any of the *Karate Kid* movies. In the original, Ralph Macchio portrays a young impetuous American teenager who wants to learn karate all at once. Pat Morita plays the *sensei* (master) who directs the student to wax his vehicle. The student becomes incensed with the continual insistence of the sensei to "wax on, wax off," an unrelenting and seemingly unrelated activity. The repetitive motion becomes one of those learned behaviors that the student ends up relying on during actual combat. Wax on, wax off, a defensive maneuver, became the first kata learned by the student. This is precisely how human beings learn.[16] Failure, practice, perfecting, and most of all patience are at the heart of any skill development. It is no different teaching a manager the appropriate application of plan–do–check–act (PDCA) within a kata during their daily improvement or problem-solving activities. In the movie, the impulsive nature of the student had to be conquered, not by the sensei but by the student's own submission to the kata.

During World War II, the U.S. War Manpower Commission developed the Training Within Industry (TWI) program from which three of the Seven Kata are derived.[16] The American statistician Walter A. Shewhart developed PDCA from which the three kata of *Toyota Kata* have evolved and which have only recently been recognized by Mike Rother.[18,19] These methods are all American! Yet it seems that the Japanese are credited with leveraging their power.

We two authors teach many variations of the PDCA cycle as applied to project management, problem solving, and improvement activities. As such, our interpretation of PDCA had typically revolved around its use as a directional rudder. Our access to NIST-MEP training has exposed us to the importance of rapid PDCA cycling by the innovation engineering methods espoused by Doug Hall. One of Hall's familiar quips, "fail fast, fail cheap," is a concept that is in total agreement with the Improvement Kata introduced in Chapter 2.[20] It is no coincidence that both Hall's innovation engineering and Rother's Improvement Kata stress the importance of the successive rapid cycling of PDCA. We now clearly understand the connection between innovation and improvement; they are essentially one and the same. Thus, we recognize the applicability of the Improvement Kata to innovation efforts as an entirely underappreciated feature of Lean. It then should be no surprise why the Toyota Prius was developed so many years ahead of its competition.[21]

We authors, as TMAC (Texas Manufacturing Assistance Center) field staff, are charged with providing world-class manufacturing practices to Texas's manufacturing base. As such, we've had the unique opportunity of working with a wide variety of organizations. We have worked with multinational corporations that employ in the thousands. We have also worked with family and closely held businesses. Working with a two-person operation isn't uncommon, and we've often worked in industry sectors outside of manufacturing. In more than 25 years of combined industrial extension experience, we have noted the similarities of organizations that seem to easily adopt and successfully exploit best practices and contrasted them to those that never try, stumble, or even give up. By understanding these successes and failures, we acutely appreciate the immediate need for organizations to learn the way of kata.

Leadership is number one. Leadership alone, however, will not suffice. Willingness is important, but learning the seemingly contradictory skills of constructive change and responsible preservation takes more than mandate.

The skills of changing (improvement kaizen) and preservation (maintenance kaizen) must be taught uniformly and then practiced daily by management.[22] In the chapters that follow, we will explain what role each of the kata play within this concept of a kaizen duality. We also submit that all Seven Kata, to varying degrees, are a vital part of leader standard work.[23]

Essential elements for success are often boiled down to enlightened leadership, and uniform methods of standardization and improvement. Fortunately, the Seven Kata provide a robust assortment of replicable practices that can quickly achieve simultaneous adaptability and conformity within management's ranks. Managers must master the disparate skills of adaptability and conformity first. Only then will they be able to use both synergistically.

Lean practices have traditionally been considered to be an extension of Japanese manufacturing techniques in general and elements of the Toyota Production System in particular. Recognizing the advancement of adaptable behavior patterns of these techniques while ignoring the national historical culture of religious syncretism and ritual practice from which they emanated can keep us from fully understanding the "unseen of Lean."

To understand the application of the Seven Kata, a thumbnail depiction of Japanese history is in order.

1.4 Training Within Industry's Japanese Connection

During one of our TWI train-the-trainer trainings, Conrad once mentioned to our sensei, Patrick Graupp, that it was good that the Japanese were the ones to conserve TWI because "everything is a ceremony with the Japanese." Patrick just chuckled. This is an important nuance not to be missed! The TWI courses are for the most part scripted. In today's PowerPoint-driven training environment, modern training delivery often seems to rely on a cue that a slide may provide the trainer. If more than one trainer uses the same slide deck, learning is dependent on that trainer's interpretation and level of expertise. Nothing was ever left to chance when the TWI courses were developed in the early 1940s.

"Sticking to the script" was a major directive given to all World War II–era TWI instructors and is still advocated today by the TWI Institute.[24] The original World War II training material even states at the bottom of each page, "Do not commit to memory, follow the script."[25] Interestingly, one of our interpretations of kata implies practice, very much a component of effective script delivery. Any experienced TWI instructor will quickly make the connection between their experiences delivering the scripted training of the courses and the concept of kata.

Being collectively party to 10 TWI train-the-trainer sessions, we've witnessed prospective trainers try to do it their way, without the benefit of reading the script. In one session, when asked to deliver a certain portion of the Job Relations training, a fellow trainee told senior master trainer Patrick Graupp, "I've trained employees for over 25 years, and I'm not about to start boring them to tears by reading to them!" Patrick calmly invited him to do it the way he felt was best. To this fellow's chagrin, in trying to skim the material as he spoke, he tripped himself up numerous times and even read remarks he had prematurely mentioned. After stumbling through the section, this experienced trainer, new to TWI, immediately understood his mistake and mentioned to Patrick, "I'm going to have to brush up on my out-loud reading skills."

The Japanese "ritualization," or strict adherence to the script, was what has preserved TWI's exacting standards. Exacting training standards is what makes TWI so effective. Ironically, reconstitution of TWI to or above World War II standards might have been impossible without the help of our previous wartime enemy's safeguarding of this important component of organizational technology.

Conrad's original remark to Patrick about TWI's 50-year conservation by the Japanese isn't that far off the mark. As it turns out, Japan was probably the best place in which TWI training could have simultaneously blossomed while still being preserved. In fact, it was also used sparingly in Europe for the Marshall Plan but didn't last much into the 1950s.[26] Japan is demonstrably a syncretistic culture with more than its share of ritualistic customs. Both syncretism and ritualism have played the essential role in the development and practice of the Seven Kata.

1.5 Lean's Formula: Syncretism and Ritual

Through much of the Far East history, China has traditionally been at the center of religion, culture, and technology. Japan had historically been at the periphery of their known world. You must stand in China or Korea, west of Japan, to be in "the Land of the Rising Sun."

As such, Japan has always thrived by duplicating foreign technology, refining it, and eventually integrating it into their culture. This is as true of Japan's dual religions of Shintoism and Buddhism, as it is of their reputation as first adopters of technology, fashion, and the arts.[27] Syncretism goes hand in hand with adaptability. To adopt an alien concept and integrate it into one's own tradition is a powerful socioeconomic strategy—one that the United States has also demonstrated dexterous ability in.

Another important component of Japanese culture that lends itself to socioeconomic aptitude is the role of rituals. A ritual is procedure's affluent cousin. A deft application of procedure is the foundation of any healthy operation. Procedures enable standardization, a bulwark of Lean. Standardization is the first order of business in business. Every culture, nonetheless, has ritual. It is a part of being human. Rituals calm and focus thought, enabling reflection. Rituals are kata. They teach and standardize the transfer of knowledge and skill, precisely the life-blood of competitive twenty-first century economic warriors.

Even a superficial grasp of Japanese culture can help us recognize the lucrative social practices that the kata bring to organizational management. The syncretistic and ritualistic aspects of ancient Japanese culture may have fostered the practice of kata within some Japanese organizations. The important distinction here is that even if kata were inherent, all Japanese organizations have not demonstrated some unique superior ability to leverage this perceived cultural advantage.

As business consultants, trainers, and coaches we feel it necessary to help dispel the myth that Lean management works for the Japanese because it is in accordance with some intrinsic cultural trait. Nothing could be further from the truth. The mindset of "here in America, we think differently; we're more 'individualistic'" is all too often accepted as a cogent argument in criticism of Lean. Such thoughts are anathema to this book's thesis.

Instead of trying to circumvent discussion with our customers by "Americanizing" Lean terminology, we feel it important to enhance understanding through a historical perspective. Japanese syncretism was fought for and could have just as easily been lost if not for the foresight and courage of a very few. We, therefore, will add a bit more granularity on how technological syncretism became a cultural force in Japan, and most of all, why.

Necessity is the mother of invention. Japan was pulled kicking and screaming into the industrial age by the navies of Great Britain, the United States, the Netherlands, and France. If it wasn't for the fall of the Tokugawa military junta (the bakufu) in 1868, Japan could have just as easily ended up in a situation that might have more closely resembled China's nineteenth and early twentieth century history. The adoption of Western technology not only granted Japan autonomy, but is also responsible for Japan's ability to colonize much of the Far East early in the twentieth century leading up to World War II.

It seems that in 1863, five samurai of the Choshu clan began to recognize the value of Western technology, especially in application to its weapons of war.[28] They were very much against opening up to the West and believed that they could learn about the needed technologies and bring them back to Japan for their own use. The bakufu, as wary as they were of the West, began to allow more trade and Western contacts. They, however, confined all Western trade to three ports and maintained close watch over transactions. This perceived kowtowing infuriated the Choshu as well as other southern Japanese clans.

The Choshu Five, as they became known, decided to risk their lives and left home to investigate how the industry and technology of the West might be used in the defense of Japan against the West. Their curiosity was neither appreciated nor sanctioned and the bakufu shogunate would have had them beheaded if caught.

All five of the intrepid samurai made their way to England, where they were accepted into academic circles. They were introduced to the industrial technologies that had originally piqued their interests. In fact, three of the five remained for some time and studied at University College London, England's only nondenominational university at the time. They began to appreciate the fact that Japan could not easily adopt the weapons and technology it desired. These samurai warriors finally came to understand Japan's need to develop its own skill and knowledge infrastructure to guarantee its continued autonomy.

While in England, the Choshu samurai learned that some southern Japanese clans, including the Choshu, were firing on Western ships sailing between Japanese islands. Two of the five returned immediately upon the news and were luckily able to get back into Japan, heads intact, and warn the clans of the futility of confronting the West. They were able to convince the clans that a full-throated confrontation with the West could lead to the colonization, or worse, partitioning of Japan by one or more of the Western powers.

The southern clans came to understand that the bakufu shogunate's policy of controlled appeasement while neglecting technological syncretism was a formula for disaster. A civil war broke out, and the Choshu clan ended up on the winning side that dismantled the shogunate. The teenage emperor was reinstated, and Meiji Japan was born.

The Choshu Five all became either politicians or captains of industry. They ushered in the reemergence of Emperor Meiji's unifying presence and a headlong rush into industrial and technological syncretism. They realized early on that the ramifications of only maintaining their artistic and cultural wealth without adopting technology as a defense from the West could mean the end of Japan as a nation.[29]

Realize that in the beginning, the Choshu samurai were in the minority. Most Japanese were skeptical of Western technology before coming to the realization that technology really couldn't be kept at arm's length. Ironically, we sometimes make the same arguments to some of our less-sophisticated customers that the Choshu Five made to their clan some 150 years ago.

Even in highly homogeneous societies like Japan, ideas on how best to remain homogeneous can be different, not to mention the varied philosophies of those that desire to be different. This is why not every Japanese organization operates at world-class levels. We're not even sure that Toyoda, Ohno, and Shigeo Shingo consciously realized that the syncretism and ritualism inherent in their own culture might provide some level of competitive advantage for Toyota. The *Toyota Kata* has, however, helped us recognize the need for all organizations to adopt business versions of syncretism and ritual. We propose that Lean's Seven Kata can be a tailor-made starting point.

The Seven Kata represent the means by which an organization can begin making continual improvements. Application of the Seven Kata cultivates the adaptive learning crucial for the acceptance of improvements. The Seven Kata system is symbiotic with learning complementing process improvement, which in turn complements more learning. All it takes is every manager in your organization putting 15 minutes of focused improvement effort into his or her daily schedule. Much like golf, performing a daily kata is conceptually simple, but in no sense is consistency easy.

1.6 Getting Started

A caveat to knowing that these seven skill sets are required for creating a Lean culture is in trying to understand how to facilitate their deployment. The task becomes complex when considering other Lean cultural traits such as leader standard work, daily accountability, visual management, and gemba walks.[30] The situation becomes even more byzantine when considering which Lean tools will dovetail with the learned skills. Cultural traits, thinking skills, and organizational tools all combine into a dizzying confluence of complexity. Practices must be ingrained, skills must be practiced, and tools must be appropriately chosen. Is it any wonder that so many organizations lose their way on their Lean journey?

After an organization has decided to begin their Lean journey in earnest, our suggested starting point for the process begins with the performance of a system-wide value stream analysis (VSA).[31] From this, improvements can be prioritized and the required skills identified.

The skills most often required for the performance of improvement kaizen are improvement and instructional skills. Improvement Kata will need to be performed on an ongoing (daily) basis, and changes in task performance will require on-the-job training (OJT) as needed. The rates of instructional and improvement kata skill development and applicability are dissimilar; this should be taken into account. In essence, novice Improvement Kata practitioners will almost immediately start providing improvement initiatives, some of which will require instructional skills to standardize. Proper OJT skill, on the other hand, takes time and practice to perfect. If the improvement is made without a capability to properly standardize it, it will be largely ineffective.

Visual controls, error proofing, and mistake proofing (poke yoke) are other important tools whose applications must be fully considered when standardizing kata improvements. However, because these techniques are not kata, they are outside the scope of this book.

To us then, before conducting the VSA, the longer process of building the instructional skills of management should begin. The TWI Job Instruction (JI) training and subsequent practice of its kata(s) by an advanced team should be conducted post haste. It will take at least a month if not more of daily practice to develop the first crop of managers armed with the skill of JI. From that group, a JI trainer for the entire organization should be chosen. The trainer should be sent to JI train-the-trainer training and be afforded the opportunity to begin practicing delivery of the course in such a way that it paces JI course deliveries to the actual demand for its use.

While some level of instructional proficiency is being reached, the VSA should be conducted. As will be fully explained in Chapter 2, the development of a future state vision is necessary for the alignment of Improvement Kata activities. The areas targeted by the future state map for improvement will identify who should begin learning the Improvement Kata first. JI OJT trainers need to be at the ready when Improvement Kata cycling begins.

1.7 A Word of Warning to Top Management

Chapter 4 details the development of the organization's preceptors. Executive management should skip ahead and read that section first. From our experience, we have witnessed far too many directors, vice presidents, and organizational officers who have come to believe that they "have arrived" and were hired into their positions specifically to bestow their pearls of wisdom down the chain of command. If you, as the officer of the organization, cannot spend the time necessary to practice a daily kata, don't be surprised at your wasted efforts in becoming Lean.

It is our sincere aspiration that the reader's eyes will be opened to the realization that for their organization to duplicate some of Toyota's successes, they must not attempt to copy tools and techniques, but rather imbue their workforce with the proper set of skills. These are the weapons of the economic warrior.

Chapter 2

Improvement Kata: Kaizen

2.1 Means to an End—Kata and Kaizen

Kaizen has always been the enigmatic soul of Lean. There are as many different definitions of kaizen as there are Lean practitioners. If, for the sake of argument, we define kaizen as continuous improvement, we know most organizations don't require the workforce to perform improvement activities continuously—on a daily basis. So, even though the Lean community has bandied kaizen about for almost 30 years, it is more often than not an unachieved aspiration.

Two similar and equally important components of the *Toyota Kata* are the Improvement Kata and the Problem-Solving (PS) Kata. As will be explained in Chapter 5, the PS Kata is descended from the Practical Problem Solving training and is also an antecedent of Toyota's current Toyota Business Practices (TBP) training.[1]

We believe the Improvement Kata to be the heart and soul of improvement kaizen. The Improvement Kata focuses only on improvement and disregards the entire causal analysis process. Problem analysis is lengthy, complex, and often, negative. Improvement efforts are composed of brief experiments and creative inspiration. Thus, the Improvement Kata is not only the means of improvement kaizen; it is also Lean's cultural modifier.[2]

To be clear, two types of kaizen exist and fit elegantly into a more complete understanding of the Seven Kata. This chapter explains the inexorable link between the Improvement Kata and improvement kaizen. Maintenance kaizen is defined as efforts to eliminate, once and for all, adverse occurrences that are encountered during the course of normal operations, or more colloquially, Murphy's Law.[3] The majority of the other Seven Kata are in one way or another different forms of maintenance kaizen. The remainder of this chapter will focus on improvement, which seeks to raise the performance bar of a motivated management team.

Consider your organization and ask yourself two questions: (1) Does your entire organization's behaviors reflect the ideals found in the Lean literature, and (2) does every lead, supervisor, manager, director, vice-president, and officer participate in daily improvement activities? As will be made abundantly clear throughout this book, affirmation of the latter determines the success of the former.

Any organization seeking the benefits of Lean must have a comprehensive understanding of the previous paragraph. The Improvement Kata, as described in *Toyota Kata*,[4] is not only the required first step on a Lean journey, but it is also the requirement for all the successive steps on that journey.

Improvement kaizen is optimally conducted as follows: by all, on a daily basis, where the work is performed, in a friendly collaborative manner. The Improvement Kata will be shown to meet the stated improvement kaizen criteria. The Improvement Kata is the means to improvement kaizen.

We both participated in one of Mike Rother's Toyota Kata training events in Ann Arbor, Michigan.[5] For a complete treatment of the Improvement Kata, a general study of the book *Toyota Kata* and the *Improvement Kata & Coaching Kata Handbook* specifically is in order. Our intention is not to reinvent, radically change, or even replicate the excellent practices Rother has developed. After actually using the methods, we have become so convinced of the Improvement Kata efficacy that we believe every employee in a Lean organization who oversees the work of others should know and practice the Improvement Kata daily.

What follows is based on our interpretation and practice of the Practical Problem Solving method introduced in *Toyota Kata* and the Improvement Kata training that we received from Mike Rother. The PS Kata was our first foray into the practice of a kata, which we then supplemented with Rother's training. We then initiated our practice of the Improvement Kata in an operation.

Performing the PS Kata before attempting the use of the Improvement Kata was beneficial. The PS Kata reaffirmed our appreciation for the substantial efforts required for effective problem solving. Since the PS Kata and the Improvement Kata are so similar, it made us aware of the rigor and due diligence that would be required for properly performing the Improvement Kata. Compared with the PS Kata, however, the Improvement Kata is fun. Instead of dealing with the slow pace and negativity that can sometimes come with problem solving, the Improvement Kata provides the practitioner positive experiences in goal setting, rapid cycles of experimentation, and a spirit of blamelessness.

2.2 Value Stream Analysis

In preparation for the use of the Improvement Kata, the organization must ensure that the improvements to be made are in alignment with one another. To accomplish this, a value stream analysis should be performed. The future state value stream map is used to focus the efforts of the various Improvement Kata on the prioritized processes.

After the current state value stream map has been developed, codependent processes within the value stream are identified and grouped into *value stream loops*.[6] Depending on each of their particular circumstances, some of these loops may provide opportunities for flow, leveling, or pull. Regardless, each loop will require alterations.

In our following example, we will consider the pacemaker loop. The pacemaker loop is also described as the system's constraint. A system may exhibit many bottlenecks, but its constraint is the bottleneck that ultimately determines system capacity.[7]

This is why Improvement Kata activities should initially target the value stream's pacemaker loop (Figure 2.1). Say the future state vision for the pacemaker loop is one-piece flow. Improvement efforts must begin by focusing on conditions within the pacemaker loop that hinder one-piece flow. Once the future state map is available, it should be used as the compass that directs the way of the Improvement Kata.

In our upcoming example (see Section 2.3.2.1), if the vision is one-piece flow, during the Improvement Kata the practitioner will produce a current condition process map (block diagram) of the pacemaker that exposes obstacles to one-piece flow. This idealized mental model can be evoked as the Improvement Kata initial framing questions are considered. Often, however, block diagrams will reveal a current state whose current conditions must then be dealt with individually.

Each new current condition requires the subsequent determination of a new target condition (challenge). So, even though a high-level systemwide

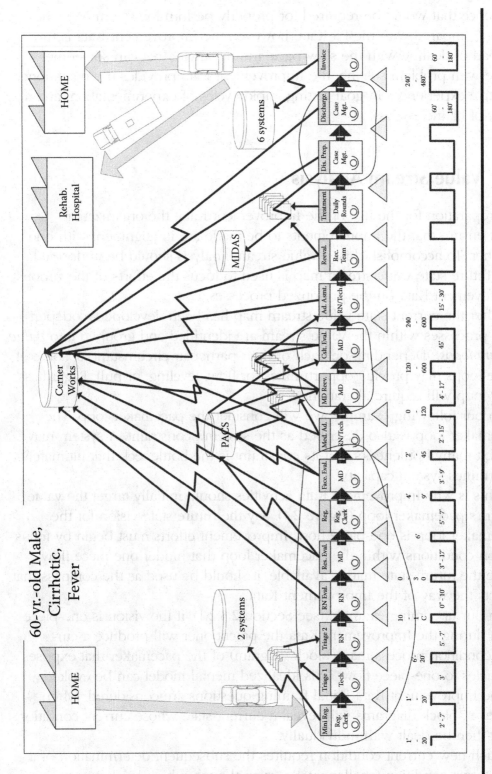

Figure 2.1 Example of a current state, value stream map with loops.

value stream map can provide a vision for Improvement Kata alignment, it's the repeated iteration of the kata focused on one area that surfaces relevant smaller-scale task and process-level target conditions. These newly found target conditions (challenges) can then be dealt with individually.

Unlike the PS Kata, whose scope is defined by a problem that has surfaced, multiple Improvement Kata activities require the vision and direction that a value stream map can provide. Random Improvement Kata activity will provide islands of improvement, but countervailing target conditions will eventually retard progress.

In the following sections, we will provide practical guidance for either practicing or coaching the Improvement Kata as depicted in Figure 2.2.

The Improvement Kata

FRAMING QUESTIONS

1. What is the target condition? (The challenge)

- What do we expect to be happening?

- List the conditions (w/out adjectives).

2. What is the actual condition now? (Go & See)

- Is the description of the current condition measurable?

◇ Block diagram, same every cycle?

◇ Takt, Cycle times, cycle times vary?

◇ Output fluctuation, 1X1 flow, staffing?

◇ Capacity/shifts, number of operators?

- List the actual conditions.

3. What obstacles are now keeping you from the target condition? Which are you addressing now?

- Compare current vs. target conditions.

- Focus on one obstacle at a time. Do not worry about finding the biggest obstacle, keep cycling fast and you'll find it.

Rev. 04   7/11

THE NEXT EXPERIMENT

4. What is your next step? (Start of next PDCA cycle)

- Take only one step at a time, but do so in rapid cycles.

- The next step does not have to be the most beneficial, biggest, or most important. Most important is that you take a step.

- Many next steps are further analysis, not countermeasures.

- If next step is more analysis, what do we expect to learn?

- If next step is a countermeasure, what do we expect to happen?

PREPARE FOR REFLECTION

5. When can we go and see what we have learned from taking that step?

- As soon as possible. Today is not too soon. How about we go and take that step now? (Strive for rapid cycles!)

15 minutes a day to a better way.

Rev. 04   7/11

Figure 2.2   Provisional version of Improvement Kata Card, Rev 04.

2.3 Improvement Kata Method

2.3.1 Coaching the Improvement Kata

For most individuals within an organization dedicated to performing any of the Seven Kata, the Improvement Kata will be their first exposure to a daily kata. The exercise must be relevant and honored by management as a vital component of the organization's overall performance. Management should therefore track Improvement Kata results and recognize incremental achievement. Not that step-function innovation that might emanate from kata activity should be ignored, but by and large, the Improvement Kata is geared toward incremental improvement—the gold standard for kaizen.

The Improvement Kata coach is a vital link to Lean's success in any organization. As in all things, the neophyte coach will make mistakes. To avoid this, Improvement Kata training is suggested for an advanced team of managers. Following any training, team coaching is advised. A coaching pair should team up, and each coach critiques the other's performance according to their training and in agreement with Rother's *Improvement Kata & Coaching Kata Handbook.*

We also suggest that the Training Within Industry (TWI) Job Instruction course be taken by anyone aiming to become a kata coach before taking Rother's Improvement Kata training. The Job Instruction course will provide a baseline from which developing kata coaches can judge each other's coaching performance. We believe that the combination of TWI Job Instruction training, Improvement Kata training, and coaching teams will create a solid foundation for the successful development of an organization's Lean culture.

As TWI instructors we always encourage our customers to use the cards that are presented in the TWI courses. The main purpose of the cards is to prevent practitioners from missing any portion of the method and to keep them on track. Due to our TWI background, the only alteration that we have made to the method we learned in Michigan is the concerted use of a detailed Improvement Kata card. At the end of the training, Mike Rother did provide us with a card that we could use for guiding our coaching cycles (Figure 2.3). We, however, saw a need for added detail. From this experience, we recommend the use of a kata card such as the one depicted previously in Figure 2.2.

The learners invariably noticed our use of the Improvement Kata card and usually requested one of their own. We told them that when we were convinced that they understood the method and would be performing the Improvement Kata on their own, they would receive a card. We would

THE FIVE QUESTIONS

1. What is your target condition here?

2. What is the actual condition now?

3. What obstacles are now preventing you from reaching the target condition? Which one are you addressing now?

4. What is your next step?
   (start of the next PDCA cycle?)

5. When can we go and see what we have learned from taking that step?

Adapted from the Improvement Kata Handbook ver. 8
2011 Mike Rother ©

Figure 2.3   5 Questions Card, adapted from the Improvement Kata & Coaching Kata Handbook ver. 8 2011 © Mike Rother.

actually hand them their card after going through a series of plan–do–check–act (PDCA) cycles toward a target condition. It wasn't surprising to discover, after our use of the card for their coaching, that earning the card became an aspiration that motivated some learners' progress.

The coach must keep in mind that the kata sessions need to be kept to less than 15 minutes per day. When management first agrees to use the Improvement Kata, we believe their consent is based on the nominal amount of daily time required. We have gone into kata sessions where the learners will mention that they have not done their homework. We make it clear to them that the 15 minutes that we're spending coaching them is for the entire kata and that homework or more time is not specifically required. We do, however, remind them of the kata requirement of daily practice.

2.3.2 Five Questions

2.3.2.1 Framing Questions

The first three of the Improvement Kata five questions serve to frame the situation for the coming series of experiments (PDCA cycles) and are therefore referred to as the *framing questions.*

The initial framing question is as follows:

What is the target condition; that is, what do we expect to be happening? (This is the challenge.)

Initially, the coach would point out the value stream loop process map. Within the five Improvement Kata questions, the coach will ask additional questions to help the learners to assess the situation. At this point, the coach would simply ask the learner, "Within any of these process steps, which ones are performing in a condition that is not conducive to one-piece flow?" The learner is then allowed to pick any one of the nonconducive process steps, as there is usually more than one.

After a process step is chosen, the coach asks the learner, "Now that we think we know where we can improve, how do you think we should proceed?" We sometimes expound, "So, what I mean is, what do you think is the first step on the card?" If the learner's guess approximates the card's intent, kudos and praise are heaped on him or her, and the target condition is identified. If the learner's guess is off the mark, the coach may say something to the effect of, "That's a logical answer," or even, "That's a pretty good guess, but the card says..."

The coach can then ask the learner to consider what the work *pattern* might look like when the target condition is reached. We usually talk about workflow, people's travel, paperwork, machine work, computer work, and anything that describes the condition within the work environment.

The coach should then suggest to the learner that putting thoughts on paper is often helpful and then have them describe the target condition either in the form of a list of bullets or even in prose. Often, while developing the description of the target condition, quantitative measures are thought of; these should be included. If none are mentioned, the coach should question the learner's lack of quantitative consideration and probe for at least a percentage or even a raw number. It is important that the learner begins to understand that quantitative analysis leads to knowledge-based decision-making, which is always desirable.

At this point, the coach should ask the learner, "What do we do next according to the card?" The same type of response mentioned above is given to the learner according to their answer. We then move on to the second framing question:

What is the actual condition now?

This is an important teachable moment that the coach cannot neglect. The learner will usually start describing what is going on and might even mention problems in the area. If we are near a computer with Internet access, we'll ask the learner to type *genchi gembutsu* into a search engine.

We'll then ask them to read the first line. After they've read it out loud, we'll tell the learner, "Let's go see what's actually going on right now."

When we arrive in gemba, we'll usually wait a few minutes until we start asking the learner about their observations—but always in the context of what the decided-upon target condition is. Typically, we'll remind the learner of the measurable characteristics that were thought of in determining the target condition. The learner can then obtain those measures for the description of the current condition.

We'll then ask what they think is next on the card. The same type of affirmation is given upon their response. The card then directs the practitioner to draw a block diagram.

A block diagram of the current condition is always possible. Sometimes the learner mentions that today's condition isn't typical. Another teachable moment is at hand. We'll say something to the effect of, "In that case, it seems then to us that the process has not been standardized and is therefore an opportunity for improvement. A snapshot of today's process will serve us well." The coach must get the learner to understand that standardizing a nonstandard process is a valid improvement. The coach must not only be able to articulate why standardization is important, but also be able to identify how the organization standardizes its own practices.

When the learner has finished the block diagram, we then ask, "What's next?" By then, the learner has come to understand that we're asking what comes next in the Improvement Kata.

We then proceed to the possibility of taking measurements of the process. Even if we obtained numerical data when going to gemba, the learner is asked to consider other possible measures that we should go back and obtain. We first practiced the Improvement Kata in a healthcare environment. The typical healthcare environment is data rich, and there is always a great temptation to use computer data exclusively. Doing so would be a mistake. As coaches, it is our duty to make sure any conceivable relevant measurement that can be made in gemba should be. This is not to say that computerized information should not be used. The point here is to make sure the learner is actually getting into the workplace, observing, and measuring.

On several occasions, we identified measures needed for the kata to which the learner promptly produced a computer report containing the said metric. Frequently, upon further examination of how the data is collected, we find that it is either inaccurate or not what we are actually looking for. Such occasions provide the kata coach an opportunity to stress to the learner that to understand what is going on in the work environment, it is most important to not rely solely on information gained from information systems.

One precautionary point to be coached: make sure the learner does not ask questions of the worker while measuring the process. Workers must stop their work to answer questions, and then cycle times become inaccurate. Efforts must be made to capture data in real time.

In some nonmanufacturing environments, cycle times are extraordinarily long, or even worse, highly variable. Adjustments must be made and perhaps computerized data and information can be used. This does not mean that going to see can be disregarded. As previously mentioned, *genchi gembutsu* is a coachable Lean feature that cannot be squandered.

If cycle times aren't highly variable, we have the learner perform the analysis that is suggested in the *Improvement Kata & Coaching Kata Handbook*. The method of analysis offered is very applicable to stable cycle times and is also appropriate for many transactional processes. For further investigation, the reader is encouraged to review the *Improvement Kata & Coaching Kata Handbook*.[8]

Upon completion of the analysis, a target condition chart should be developed using the information gained from the measurement analysis of the current condition and the target condition description (see Figure 2.4). A corresponding objective in the target condition column should be listed across from each of the current condition metrics (see Figure 2.5).

At this point, the coach should ask the learner, "What's next?" The same routine response is given upon their answer. The coach then reads the third framing question on the card (a two-part question):

What obstacles are now preventing you from reaching the target condition? Which one are you addressing now?

After the learner responds, the coach should point out the obstacles between each of the line items of the comparative chart. We'll usually point out one of the items in the target condition and ask the learner, "In noticing the corresponding current condition item, what obstacle is keeping us from the target condition item?" (see Figure 2.5).

This process teaches the learner to choose an obstacle that is bound by the current and target conditions' corresponding items. If the student begins vacillating between more than one set of corresponding items, the coach should read from the card, "Focus on one obstacle at a time; do not worry too much about finding the biggest problem right away...you'll find it soon."

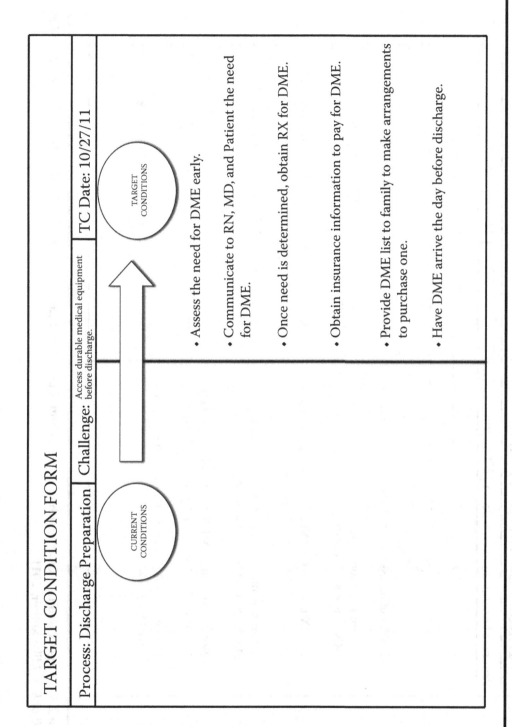

Figure 2.4 Target Condition Chart, (with examples of Target Condition), adapted from *Improvement Kata Handbook*, © Mike Rother, 2011.

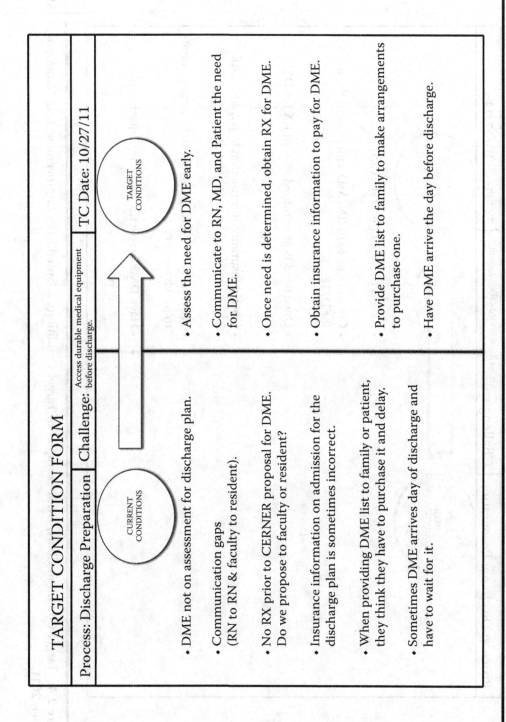

TARGET CONDITION FORM

Process: Discharge Preparation	Challenge: Access durable medical equipment before discharge.	TC Date: 10/27/11

CURRENT CONDITIONS

- DME not on assessment for discharge plan.

- Communication gaps (RN to RN & faculty to resident).

- No RX prior to CERNER proposal for DME. Do we propose to faculty or resident?

- Insurance information on admission for the discharge plan is sometimes incorrect.

- When providing DME list to family or patient, they think they have to purchase it and delay.

- Sometimes DME arrives day of discharge and have to wait for it.

TARGET CONDITIONS

- Assess the need for DME early.

- Communicate to RN, MD, and Patient the need for DME.

- Once need is determined, obtain RX for DME.

- Obtain insurance information to pay for DME.

- Provide DME list to family to make arrangements to purchase one.

- Have DME arrive the day before discharge.

Figure 2.5   Target Condition Chart (with example of both Current and Target conditions), adapted from *Improvement Kata Handbook,* © Mike Rother, 2011

Typically, the learner hasn't yet realized that the soon-to-follow rapid cycles of experimentation will eventually surface the larger obstacles. So, it is best to encourage the learner to just choose one to get started.

2.3.2.2 The Next Experiment

The learner is then asked the perfunctory, "What's next?" After guessing, the fourth question from the card is read aloud as follows:

What is your next step? (start of next PDCA cycle)

After revealing the step to the learner, we'll usually say that it's time for them to put on their scientist's hat. The coach should encourage the learner to develop a test or experiment that may overcome the obstacle. The PDCA Cycles sheet is introduced to the learner at this point (see Figure 2.6). The initial experiment is described in the Step column. The coach also has the learner fill in the column with the heading, What Do You Expect?

2.3.2.3 Prepare for Reflection

The experiment should be run as quickly as possible and the results immediately gathered. Each experiment on the way to the target condition should optimally take a 15-minute session and not much more. The coach asks the learner for the next step and qualifies their response by reading the fifth and final question from the card to the learner:

When can we go and see what we have learned from taking that step?

Strive for rapid cycles: "As soon as possible. Today is not too soon. How about we go and take that step now?"

The push for immediate results is an important detail that the coach cannot overlook. Emphasis needs to be made that the implementation of the solution is not necessarily the main point of the experiment, but rather, what is learned is of overriding significance.

Occasionally, the learner decides on an experiment that can take days or even a week or two to conclude. The coach must dissuade the learner from such an experiment and focus on a smaller segment that will not take as long to finish. Long experiments will disrupt the rapid cycling necessary for imprinting adaptive behavior patterns and is the antithesis of improvement kaizen. Another concern of lengthy experiments is that the learner is waiting for results and not participating in their daily kata. A coach's acquiescence in allowing the suspension of a daily kata not only kills momentum

PDCA Cycles Form

Process: Proposal of DME (durable medical equipment)

Process Metric: Time to sign DME (mins.)

Trial Dates	Trial/Test	What Do I Expect?	Result	What Did I Learn?
10/28	Ask CERNER power user if proposal DME is sent to faculty, can resident sign?	The proposal sent to named MD will be the one signing the proposal (i.e., faculty).	Proposal is to the MD that needs to sign. May propose to 2 residents; whoever accepts can sign for the DME.	Don't send to faculty. Send proposal to the 2 residents. The first to sign eliminates the other proposal (i.e., will not cause a "floating order" in CERNER).
10/31	Send proposal for DME to 2 residents and see what happens.	Make sure they receive and accept it. Expect to have to train them on how.	Proposal was received on MD's messages center. Showed them how to click OK and send to print on prescription printer.	Learned proposal goes to MD message center on CERNER.
11/1	Ask CERNER power user, "Can DME proposal be chosen for multiple DME devices or one per each?"	I predict that I'll be able to propose multiple devices on a single proposal.	Attempted to send multiple DMEs on a single proposal. Power user was present.	Unsuccessful.
11/2	E-mail top CERNER power user to find out if there's a way to send multiple DMEs on a single proposal.	I predict that there is a way to accomplish this.		

Figure 2.6 PDCA Cycles form.

but also sends the wrong message to the learner. Daily incremental learning, improvement, or both must be the organization's mandate to all managers!

After the experimental results are analyzed, the coach should have the learner fill in the Result and What We Learned columns on the PDCA cycle sheet (Figure 2.6).

The coach then asks the learner, "So what's next?" The learner should by this time be able to guess that another experimental cycle (repeat of questions 3 and 4) is called for. The experimental cycles should then proceed onward to the target condition.

The coach should be experienced enough to estimate how long it will take the learner to reach the target condition. The target condition should be reached within a week or two (assuming five daily kata per week). If the target condition is too aggressive and takes much longer than the two-week horizon, momentum can be lost and the experimentation is probably taking too long.

Mike Rother has mentioned that coaching is the "knob that can be turned"[9] if results are not forthcoming. In essence, Rother is telling us to get tough with the coaching and go easy on the learners. It is the coaches' responsibility to keep the kata suitable and on track. If the kata cycles are too extensive or stray from the value stream vision, the coaching needs reevaluation.

2.4 Yokoten

At first glance, *yokoten* is a Japanese term meaning technology transfer. Its practice, however, is much more involved. *Yokoten* is short for *yokoni tenkaisuru*, which means to unfold or open out sideways.[10] When we instruct certain TWI courses, more often than not the problem of poor communication is brought up. The unimpeded flow of information should be the highest aspiration of any world-class organization. Yokoten, like visual controls and Job Instruction Kata, is one of many Lean tools that enhances organization-wide communication.

During our experiences coaching the Improvement Kata, we have witnessed the development of yokoten-type communication mechanisms, first within a single department and eventually between departments. As mentioned previously in this chapter, we performed Problem-Solving (PS) Kata activities before attempting to coach the Improvement Kata. During that excursion, a PS Kata causal analysis identified a lack of department-wide communication as the point of cause for other issues. More comprehensive shift-change meetings and a better organized and visually appealing communication board were developed as countermeasures.

Soon after initiating Improvement Kata activities, an obstacle to one of the target conditions was the unawareness of improvements being worked on by different shifts. The experiment conducted consisted of posting PDCA cycle sheets so that the entire department could consider the different improvements that had been or were in the process of being addressed.

Value adders, supervisors, and managers alike began reviewing each others' Improvement Kata activities, which were then transferred to other shifts as Improvement Kata.

2.5 Conclusions

Unlike the self-scoping nature of the PS Kata, Improvement Kata activities must be aligned through the development of a value stream map. After each of the value stream loops is analyzed and the appropriate vision for each of the loops is decided upon, management has a decision to consider: Should a team-approach kaizen improvement event be planned and executed with the follow-up of continued Improvement Kata activities, or should Improvement Kata activities proceed without the benefit of a kaizen event?

This decision should be made based on how variable the cycle times are. Stable cycle times can lend themselves to appreciable improvements made through the application of a kaizen event. Any shortcomings experienced during or after the implementation can be dealt with through the application of the Improvement Kata.

Variable cycle times, which are more common in the service sector, can present vexing challenges to team-based improvements. In such cases, we suggest the use of a "divide and conquer" strategy that many managers using the Improvement Kata simultaneously can apply. The trial-and-error incremental progress made toward target conditions aligned to the value stream loop vision is the most efficient method for making gains in this type of environment.

Kaizen events can be an effective way to make large gains, but use of the Improvement Kata independent of team-based efforts bridges the gaps between punctuated events.

Chapter 3

Nested Job Instruction Kata: Learn to Teach

We have learned that the Training Within Industry (TWI) courses' implications go well beyond the limited name that they bear, that is, *training*. Accordingly, one should not assume that by merely sending an employee to Job Instruction (JI) training, a competent trainer is created. Training alone is never enough. Treated as awareness training, JI is not worth the expense of its cost in tuition and loss in employee time. Knowing about a world-class method has no value if not applied. An enigmatic factor of the proper application of JI training is the performance of a JI Kata. We will explain what the nested JI Kata are and how they work synergistically to create a world-class on-the-job trainer. Using JI, this chapter also lays out a plan for transforming from the traditional fiat-driven organization to the learning organization that Lean requires.

For far too long, managers have been using the buddy system to train employees. What follows is a scenario that is similar to those we've witnessed in countless organizations.

Bill was a new employee. On the first day of work, Julie, the human resources specialist, met Bill in the lobby. From there, Julie escorted Bill to her office where she had Bill fill out some forms and answered his questions. From there, Julie took Bill to the training room, where he was met by the company trainer. The company trainer took Bill and some other new employees through the company orientation. Bill was then treated to lunch at the company cafeteria.

After lunch, Julie met Bill and took him to meet his new supervisor. After some initial pleasantries, Julie left and Bill was taken out to the plant floor for a tour. After the tour, Bill's supervisor introduced him to Agatha. Bill's supervisor told him, "Bill, Agatha is our best operator. Today I want you to go back with Agatha to her workstation and just observe what she does. Tomorrow morning, Agatha will start formally training you. Now if you have any questions, be sure to ask Agatha; she knows it all."

On Bill's second day of work, he met up with Agatha, and she meticulously explained everything related to the work that Bill would be performing. All the while, Agatha asked Bill, "Do you have any questions?" Bill rarely had questions, but did ask a few. After lunch, Agatha had Bill perform the work and corrected him as they went along. By the end of the day, Agatha evaluated Bill's performance and reported to the supervisor that Bill was "trained up."

Some smaller operations might consider that the scenario just described is more than they do when initiating a new employee. The typical organization, however, would probably agree that their training follows the same pattern as described. Well, if this training narrative resembles your organization's training method in the least bit—you are absolutely, precisely, positively training employees inappropriately. You should consider defects that recur and those made by new employees a result of your neglectful training practices.

Even though JI on-the-job training (OJT) is the only method that can deliver consistently superior training results, at an almost visceral level, insecure learners may relate your training to the grading systems that we were all subject to in school. The onus for first-time quality cannot be on an unsure employee; it belongs to us as managers. As repeatedly stated in unison with participants of the JI course, "If the worker hasn't learned, the instructor hasn't taught." In business, anything less than perfect means added cost, or worse yet, a dissatisfied customer. Of course, employees do eventually catch on; but as JI assures us, relying on each employee's initial level of acumen is not a sure and reliable method.

"There is, however, a sure and reliable method that works every time, if followed. This method is the Training Within Industry Job Instruction (TWI-JI) training." These words are straight out of the TWI-JI instructor's manual, and no truer words were ever written.[1] The caveat, however, is "works every time, if followed." Some may believe that if they take the course, they will be prepared to deliver an excellent OJT. The problem with that assumption is that the JI method is a skill that takes practice to master.

If the JI OJT is to be given, it is advisable that the OJT trainer masters the method to keep from confusing the learner. Mastery of JI OJT through the practice of the JI Kata is addressed at the end of this chapter.

3.1 Training to Instruct

We will first highlight breakthroughs in the evolution of OJT up to the current state of the art, TWI-JI. Our focus is directed at convincing you, the reader, that a standardized OJT program based on TWI-JI is one of the baseline requirements for creating a Lean culture.

In an industrial setting, economic stability and organizational flexibility are of eminent importance. We will explain how to achieve superior organizational flexibility as a hedge against economic uncertainty. This entire book is dedicated to rendering a straightforward path that management can follow—one that, in this chapter, is also easily applied whenever your staff needs training for their work. An employee's initial orientation is the only first impression the organization will ever get to imprint the organization's standard of excellence on their employee. This same principle of learning while on the job is used in the previous chapter's treatment of the Improvement Kata quest to standardize the improvement process. Developing your manager's skills is one of your most important jobs; and each of these skills, including instruction, needs to be taught correctly the first time. Let's quickly review how not to train.

How should new employees, including managers, be trained? Should training begin with the assignment of a mentor for the trainee, someone with experience and who knows the job the best? Should the training continue with shadowing and an informal stream of explanations, questions, and answers? Is the training culminated when the allotted training time has expired? These are all indicators of a poorly considered OJT program and is much like the scenario described above. We may think ourselves a new and more knowledgeable generation, but in such a basic practice as OJT, more organizations than not are easily 500 years behind what is currently known about OJT. This error is possibly made from the mistaken assumption that OJT should be modeled directly after the age-old practice of apprenticeship. After all, apprenticeship is the one-to-one tutelage of a student by a master. This is a logical, but incorrect, presumption.

3.1.1 On-the-Job Training Development

The roots of OJT can indeed be found in the long-standing practice of apprenticeship. The similarities, however, end there. The craft guilds of Renaissance Europe developed apprenticeship into a system of collaborative competition that generated social and technological advancement as well as high art. Apprenticeship provided young boys an early path to self-sufficiency. As an aside, it also produced masters like Michelangelo and Leonardo da Vinci. Apprenticeship was a bottom-up learning experience that could easily last 10 years. By the time a journeyman became a master, society would have produced a technological and economic engine not easily replaced.[2]

The apprenticeship system had many strengths; its major weakness was the amount of time it took an individual to reach full development. A master's base of skill and knowledge was both deep and wide, but was not easily passed on to others. The nontransportability of skills and knowledge constrained the ability of technology to grow at the exponential rates that are now common. It wasn't until the industrial revolution, with the advent of machine work and the disaggregation of labor, that the need for a deep understanding of specialized knowledge overtook the need for a vast array of personal skill. To compete in our day and age, skill is now a focused effort, and the speed of skill acquisition is of the essence. To be clear, the focused skills needed today must be flawless. The breadth, however, of highly specialized skills within a single individual need not be as broad as in the past. Given advances in technology as well as teaching methods, we can now achieve production and service levels unparalleled in history. For most organizations, technological advances are capital intensive and highly dependent on their supplying original equipment manufacturers (OEMs). The way we teach and train employees, however, is the most practical and relatively inexpensive means of enhancing production and service requirements. This is what we will focus on here.

Johann Friedrich Herbart (1776–1841), the father of scientific pedagogy, played the first historical role in the development of JI. In his work *Universal Pedagogy*,[3] Herbart identified five steps in teaching:

1. Preparation: relating new material to be learned to relevant existing knowledge
2. Presentation: imparting the new material concretely with actual experience
3. Association: connecting existing knowledge to new knowledge

4. Generalization: taking the learned experience into the realm of abstract thought

5. Application: testing the new knowledge to ensure its understanding

The JI four-step method of training a worker is depicted in Figure 3.1. A comparison of JI's four steps to Herbart's five steps reveals an interesting relationship. Step 1 in the JI method is, "Prepare the worker." It is identical to Herbart's first step. Herbart's step 3, association, is integrated into JI's step 1 as indicated by the subhead, "Find out what the learner already knows." In the JI course, it is made clear that this subhead is important in qualifying the learner who might not have the proper background to pick up learning from the lesson that they were about to receive. Conversely, it can also help the trainer assess if the learner has advanced beyond the instruction to be given.

JOB INSTRUCTION
HOW TO GET READY TO INSTRUCT

Before Instructing people how to do a job:

1. MAKE A TIME TABLE FOR TRAINING
Who to train
For which work...
By what date...

2. BREAK DOWN THE JOB
List **Important Steps**
Select **Key Points**
Safety factors are always Key Points

3. GET EVERYTHING READY
The proper equipment, tools, materials and whatever needed to aid instruction

4. ARRANGE THE WORKSITE
Neatly, as in actual working conditions

TWI
Institute
www.TWI-Institute.org

4 STEPS FOR JOB INSTRUCTION

Step 1 - PREPARE THE WORKER
• Put the person at ease
• State the job
• Find out what the person already knows
• Get the person interested in learning the job
• Place the person in the correct position

Step 2 - PRESENT THE OPERATION
• Tell, show and illustrate one **Important Step** at a time
• Do it again stressing **Key Points**
• Do it again stating **reasons for Key Points**
Instruct clearly, completely and patiently but don't give them more information than they can master at one time

Step 3 - TRY OUT PERFORMANCE
• Have the person do the job--correct errors
• Have the person explain each **Important Step** to you as they do the job again
• Have the person explain each **Key Point** to you as they do the job again
• Have the person explain **reasons for Key Points** to you as they do the job again
Make sure the person understands. Continue until you know they know

Step 4 - FOLLOW UP
• Put the person on their own
• Designate who the person goes to for help
• Check on the person frequently
• Encourage questions
• Taper off extra coaching and close follow-up

IF THE WORKER HASN'T LEARNED, THE INSTRUCTOR HASN'T TAUGHT

Figure 3.1   TWI Job Instruction Card, adapted from TWI-Institute.org.

Regardless, as Herbart's step 3 points out, associating the new knowledge is an important feature of learning.

Herbart's second step, presentation, is identical to JI's step 2, "Present the operation." This is the step that is invariably performed even in some of the worst of OJT. Though everyone understands that the learner must see the operation to at least begin mimicking it, it doesn't mean that the learner truly understands the job.

As mentioned above, Herbart's step 3 is addressed in the JI step 1. Herbart's step 4 is also addressed in the JI method. In both step 2, "Present the operation," and step 3, "Apply the method," the learner is given the reasons for key points in step 2 and then asked to recite them in step 3. Reasons for the key points are typically abstract concepts for the learner because, without experience, the reasons for the key points are precautionary or extrapolative. Incidentally, the reasons for key points are a part of the training that seems to have been practiced in the United States during World War II but not documented on the 1940s version of the JI card.[4] The reasons for key points are now an important part of JI that Toyota emphasizes in their version of the training.[5]

Herbart's step 5, application, is covered in JI's step 3, "Apply the method." Step 3 is the test that allows the instructor an understanding of the learner's progress. In JI, step 3 consists of having the learner perform the job while identifying the important steps, key points, and the reasons for key points. JI teaches that the simultaneous demonstration of the job along with a precise description is an indicator of understanding and not just a copy of the motions.

Another important milestone in the development of JI was achieved through the work of Charles Allen (1862–1938).[6] Charles Allen was employed by the U.S. Shipping Board during World War I to develop a training program that could address the sudden demand for new ships and correspondingly the vast training needs of new shipyard workers.[7] After the war, he published the book *The Instructor, the Man, and the Job*.[8] What follows is a description from the book of his four-step method for training a worker:

1. Preparation
2. Presentation
3. Application
4. Testing

The only significant difference from Allen's four-step method and the JI four-step method is step 4. Allen's rendition is seemingly an earlier revision of the JI method. "Allen's 4-step method was the basis for all of the training programs developed and dispersed by the TWI [sic] during World War II."[9]

During our tenure as TWI-JI instructors, we have come upon employees who complain and ask, "Why do I have to announce the number of every important step and key point and also say *important step* and *key point* every time I demonstrate it?" Or, "I have my own style that works for me." Or even, "This operation is so complex that it is not conducive to this method." Every single aspect of JI was carefully vetted during its initial development and has survived more than 60 years of Japanese scrutiny. As an example, having to recite the number of the important steps and to say the words *important step* provides a mental marker within the task sequence, beneficial for aural learning. There is no room for personal style that veers away from the method. The JI method may seem rigid, but it has been shown to be flexible enough to handle the most complex of tasks. There really is no good reason to ignore the JI method once it is known.

We must consider the plain fact that everyone learns differently. For example, if the instructor's learning style is, say, visual, and the learner's is, per chance, tactile, the instructor may come to believe that this learner isn't so keen on the uptake if the learner witnessed the task executed properly but was never given the opportunity to perform the task him- or herself. Truth be told, the instructor is teaching to him- or herself and can be somewhat oblivious to any strengths or weaknesses in the learner's personal learning style. The TWI-JI method was developed to accommodate all learning styles and is therefore preferred. In fact, none of the other TWI course topics can as comprehensively account for every learning style because they're all content specific. It is our opinion that TWI-JI is the premier training needed by all organizations.

Both Herbart's and Allen's contributions drove industrial instructional technology to the apex of the national industrial output that America experienced during World War II. It has also played an integral role in the development of the post–mass production technology that we currently refer to as Lean. Considering the craft guild apprenticeship systems developed some 500 years ago, we know that current organizations don't have the luxury of developing the kinds of expansive mastery that arose then. It's about time that your organization begins training and coaching your employees in the only correct method of OJT.

3.1.2 Power of One-on-One

Unlike all other types of educational experiences, nothing can supplant the power and efficiency of the instruction by one teacher given to one student. For education, training, and coaching, one-on-one instruction is the gold standard. Seemingly, one-on-one training is extremely resource intensive and should not be as efficient as block (classroom) training. It is true that a single teacher can bring a group of students up to some level of proficiency with a few bright stars within the mix. However, with ever more expensive resources and the competitive increases in quality, recurring mistakes are becoming too costly to absorb.

We might as well accept the fact that the one and only best way to inject a new and able worker into the business environment who is ready to contribute defect free is through individualized instruction. We should also realize that the same individualized instruction should be used to correct errors and implement new behaviors within the organization. Individualized instruction can and should be the norm for any world-class operation. With the addition of a kata coach assigned to a JI training participant immediately after the course is finished, JI one-on-one OJT can become an affordable, fast, and effective way to bring employees up to world-class levels.

3.1.3 Quintessential Standard—Demonstrated

Improving without standards is problematic. First of all, some benchmark of proficiency must be set. Without a benchmark, it is difficult to see what an improvement is. Actions become random. In essence, arguments can be easily made as to which method is best; but without a benchmark, all methods are different methods, not necessarily better ones. Secondly, what is all too often missed is the impact that these nonstandard tasks have on variability. Variability overly complicates all problem-solving efforts since different methods can haunt root cause analysis, demanding more evaluation, experimentation, and time (i.e., cost) to identify and remove the many root causes. Lastly, without a standard, it is difficult to identify an abnormal occurrence. The instantaneous identification of an abnormality is crucial in containing defective products and services and minimizing rework.

Given that a benchmark can be set using JI, the second issue becomes having everyone perform tasks in a standard way that achieves the benchmark. One might question how a manager can easily recognize compliance with the current standard. With the tens, hundreds, or even thousands of different specific tasks that a single supervisor or manager must oversee, and given all of the specific nuances in any given task, monitoring employee compliance to standards can be formidable.

The TWI Job Instruction training provides a simple way of teaching and identifying conformance to any specific task. As shown in Figure 3.2, some Toyota plants have job element sheets (JESs) available in front of every operation. The JES is not meant as a work instruction for the operator, to be used while he or she works. Rather, the JES is meant as a tool for the lead, supervisor, or manager of that area. In fact, JESs are placed facing away from the operator to facilitate the manager's easy access to the information.[10]

As evidenced by Figure 3.3, the TWI Job Instruction breakdown sheet is very closely related to the JES. Important steps and key points are used to facilitate understanding as well as a way of standardizing the format. As shown, the JES can include a drawn schematic. The advantage of drawn schematics over photographs is their superior illustration of contour and the minimization of extraneous visual noise.

3.2 Nested Kata

It is important to realize that there are more kata within JI than the four-step kata. We refer to these three additional kata as *nested* since they are intertwined with the four-step kata. The three additional kata are the kata for determining important steps (IS kata), the kata for determining key points (KP kata), and the kata for "getting ready to instruct."

The nested kata should be learned simultaneously. The IS kata and the KP kata can be learned in tandem while breaking down the jobs that will be instructed. One cannot perform the four-step JI Kata without prior preparation using the IS, KP, and getting ready katas. All four kata are mutually dependent; the use of any three kata without the other is useless. The IS and KP kata are essential in properly preparing a Job Instruction breakdown, which is also a component of the kata for getting ready to instruct. Depending on the circumstances, the JI nested kata might very well be the first kata a company employee learns.

3.2.1 Important Step (IS) Kata

The identification of important steps is simple but follows a definite pattern that must be repeated for every step in the breakdown. The IS kata is

Toyota Job Element Sheet

Model:

Element:				Horn Install		Date Created	

	T		Critical			
	Y		Option			
	P		Functional			
	E		Appearance			

Procedure (How to Do)	Key Point/Reason Why	Ergo.	Created By:
1. Pick horn and gun			
2. Align bolt through horn bracket (as per diagram (1)).	• Keep 20-25 bolts in tool punch		

3. Align bolt into rad support (as per diagram (2)) and tighten.	• First hole from right fender;
	• Torque target 12 Nm
	  Minimum 10 Nm
	  Maximum 15 Nm
	• Loose or cross thread condition not allowed (see diagram (3))
		Burden	

		Time	

Revisions	Initials	Safety Key Points
		I wear your PPE, cotton gloves, safety glasses, safety shoes

Figure 3.2   Toyota job element sheet. Adapted from Dennis, Pascal, Lean Production Simplified, 2002.

JOB INSTRUCTION BREAKDOWN SHEET

IMPORTANT STEPS	KEY POINTS	REASONS
A logical segment of the operation when something happens to advance the work.	Anything in a step that might— 1. Make or break the job 2. Injure the worker 3. Make the work easier to do; i.e., "knack," "trick," special timing, bit of special information	Reasons for the key points

Figure 3.3   Job Instruction Breakdown sheet. Adapted from TWI-Institute training materials.

practiced by asking oneself a series of questions *as the job is actually performed*. The line of questioning is as follows:

Question: What have I done?
Answer: (State what was done.)
Question: Has the job advanced?
Answer: Yes (to proceed).
Question: Can this be an important step?
Answer: Yes (if the step is significant).

As one gains experience breaking down jobs, it becomes evident that the questioning takes on a form. As with any kata, the repeated experience makes the process both nuanced as well as obvious. For example, how far should I proceed in performing the job before asking, "What have I done?" What if I've proceeded too far in the job and ask, "Has the job advanced?" How significant must the advancement of the job be in order to decide, "Can this be an important step?" These questions are answered with repeated practice. When true understanding is gained through repeated practice, the questioning sequence becomes automatic while most importantly allowing considered thought to the content and instructability of the breakdown.

3.2.2 Key Point (KP) Kata

Key points are always associated with important steps. A key point is defined as any part of the important step that can make or break the job, injure the worker, or make any part of the important step easier to do. As mentioned in the trainer's manual, selecting key points is probably the most important thing in Job Instruction training.[11] As the definition indicates, the creators of JI appreciated three easily understandable qualitative parameters that are essential in performing a task correctly. This is of paramount importance in the learner's ability to leapfrog past trial-and-error experience directly to first-time quality levels.

Similar to the IS kata, the KP kata uses a line of questioning to discover what is key to performing the job correctly. The KP kata is as follows:

Recitation: The three conditions for a key point are something that could (1) make or break the job, (2) injure the worker, (3) make the work easier to do.

Question: So, why did I do it that way? What would happen if I didn't do it
that way?
Answer: So that... (explanation of reason).
Question: What condition does it meet?
Recite: Make or break? Injure the worker? Easier to do?
Answer: Identify at least one of the conditions met.

If the action meets at least one of the three conditions, it is included in
the job breakdown as a key point for that particular important step.

This kata not only provides the key points for the important step, but in
answering why the step was conducted a certain way, it provides the reason
for the key point in question.

3.2.3 Kata for How to Get Ready to Instruct

A fourth, more subtle, kata exists within JI. On the JI card opposite the four-
step method are directions on how to get ready to instruct. It contains four
points in order:

1. Make a timetable for training.
2. Break down the job.
3. Get everything ready.
4. Arrange the work site.

Making a timetable for training is a critical component of creating and managing your organization's training program. As this point is listed first under
how to get ready to instruct, the message is clear: making a timetable for
training is the first thing that should be done before JI OJT is conducted.

The TWI-JI training timetable presented in session three of the JI course
doubles as an easily understood method for practicing the JI Kata. As shown
in Figure 3.4, a manager can easily spot training needs. Figure 3.5 uses a
numerical scale in place of the checkmarks in Figure 3.4. With such a scale,
kata coaches can easily identify, first, who should receive JI OJT based on a
skills average, and second, what jobs are thinly staffed or understaffed due
to a low total proficiency average. Of course, there are many more instructional challenges when the myriad of details and resource requirements
are considered. The remainder of this chapter will direct the reader on the
development of the resource requirements and provide guidance on handling the details.

JOB INSTRUCTION TRAINING TIMETABLE

Name: ____ Jones ____
Dept.: ____ 2nd Electrical Dept. ____
Date: ____ Today's date ____

	Breakdown No.	Smith	Lark	Morse	Taylor	Massy	Peters	Baker					Changes In Production
Assembling Parts		✓	✓	✓	✓	✓	✓	✓					
Wiring		✓	✓	✓	✓								
Combing		✓	✓	✓		✓	✓						
Knot Tying	123	✓	✓	✓	✓	✓		5/12					Need 1 more worker at beginning of April
Clamping		✓	✓	✓	*	✓	✓						
Adjustment		✓	3/9	✓	4/12								
				Scheduled to retire on 4/29									
Turnover													
Work Performance													

Figure 3.4   Job Instruction Training Timetable. Adapted from TWI-Institute training materials.

JOB INSTRUCTION TRAINING TIMETABLE

Name: _____
Dept.: _____
Date: _____

	Breakdown No.	Mary S.	John D.	Javier H.	Irma K.	Susan Tanh	Billie Bob T.					Average level	Changes In Production
Task 123	123	5	0	3	4	5	1(7/9)					3	Schedule will increase in Aug
Task 445		5	0	5	0	4	0					2.3	
Task 345	345	4	5	3	4	5	0					4.5	
Task 765		3	5	4	3	1	1					2.8	
Task 723	567	0	3	3	0	1	5					2.3	
Task 801		5	0	0	0(6/15)	0	0(6/8)					1.5	
Task 879		5	3	3	0(7/1)	0	3(7/1)					2.7	
Cross trained Ranking		3.9	3.4	3	1.6	2.3	1.4						Note: 1st number is skill level 0=none, 5=highest (month/day for scheduled training)
Turnover													
Work Performance													

Figure 3.5 Job instruction training timetable.

Generally, and especially in smaller companies, proficient operators are tasked with training new employees. If this is the case in your organization, that operator needs to master his or her instructional skill by performing the JI Kata repeatedly. As a matter of individual skill development, comprehensive process standardization, and importantly the development of competent trainers within the workforce, a well-considered plan must be developed. The training timetable can be valuable to this effort.

Many organizations have had the opportunity of training key individuals in JI. Unfortunately, far too many have not developed the all-important training timetable and used it as instructed in the course. The training timetable is as critical to a great OJT program as are the four-step method and the proper breakdown of the job as explained above. Neglecting the training timetable is a fatal flaw that will precipitate the diminution of your training regime. Top managers that neglect taking the course jeopardize its power simply because they will not be able to properly prioritize resources for the effort. The lack of appreciation of what role the training timetable plays is a prime example of what can go wrong at the top.

We have already explained the importance of using a job breakdown for properly delivering instruction. We have also observed the conduct of the breakdown requiring two kata: the important step kata, and the key point kata. In getting ready to instruct, the instruction must be clear in the instructors mind. Missed steps, key points, or even not providing reasons for key points can make for a confusing or poor session with the learner. The job breakdown preparation therefore is a critical part of instructing correctly.

The third point in getting ready to instruct is getting everything ready, as in the proper work equipment, tools, materials, and whatever is needed to aid in the instruction. It obviously doesn't make sense to attempt instruction when the implements of the task are not at hand. This point is seemingly apparent; however, in our experience we have witnessed countless scheduled training sessions that were delayed, postponed, or canceled due to a lack of available instructional aides. Everyone arrived, including the individual to be trained. The job breakdown was prepared and at hand. Unfortunately, some contingency tied up an instructional aide on that day, and the training was either conducted poorly or not at all.

The fourth get-ready point is to arrange the worksite, neatly, as in actual working condition. Again, simulating the actual setting is important in providing the mental vision of what and how the task is to be performed. It is always important to remember that training in a condition unlike the actual condition may cause confusion and errors.

Every department in the organization, including the training department, should be subject to JI training and the subsequent JI Kata. JI is applicable to all areas of the organization. The JI method works just as well in manufacturing and healthcare as it does in banking and insurance. Any task requiring instruction should be promulgated using the JI method of instruction. Growing it throughout the organization, however, requires consideration of the kata for how to get ready to instruct after key individuals have taken the JI course.

3.3 From Training Course to Kata

The TWI-JI training is an unrivaled instrument of communication. Plainly, if you're going to instruct someone on anything, the JI four-step method is the only way to make certain that the learner understands it and can perform it correctly. The training, however, cannot stand alone. JI is not meant as an awareness course; it was developed to advance the performance of on-the-job training. As such, the course demands the practice of the method for all participants. TWI is marketed as a "learn by doing" experience.[12] The JI Kata directs the course participant to "keep on doing" in gemba. TWI has been described as Lean's missing link.[13] We can now dig deeper and come to understand that the kata is TWI's missing link.

Currently, many companies are providing the JI course to their employees with the realization that it is indeed quintessentially the only method for OJT. Unfortunately, many of these organizations assume that after employees have taken the course, they can automatically use the method to train others. Since using JI for OJT is an acquired skill, more practice on using the method is necessary beyond their first attempt during the course. The repeated practice of the JI four-step method is the only way to build the capability needed for using the method to its fullest. We also know that the fastest, most comprehensive method for learning the JI four-step method is by practicing the JI Kata.

The obvious answer to mastery then is practicing the JI method repeatedly, until perfected. This repeated practice cannot be scheduled through happenstance. A manager learning the JI Kata should practice the four-step method daily. For the benefit of practice, the new trainer should be provided the opportunity to retrain an expert, that is, someone competent in the task and knowledgeable of the JI method. In this way, the new trainer can get feedback on both content (job instruction breakdown) and the JI method of delivery. Better yet, a highly competent JI trainer should audit the new trainer's live delivery. The experienced trainer then has the opportunity to take notes, enabling more complete feedback for the developing trainer. Regardless, the best method is repetitive live JI OJT deliveries with a learner dependent on the instructor's training proficiency, and immediate coaching given to the JI OJT trainer after the OJT concludes.

As will be fully explained in Chapter 4, chunking is an effective method for building skill.[14] Since step 2 of JI, "Present the operation," is arguably the most difficult step of the four steps to perfect, a JI Kata coach should chunk the four steps and have the learner initially focus on step 2. We have seen many workers become adept at presenting the job in a very short period of time by gaining confidence through mastery of step 2. When followed up with only a few repetitions of practice enhanced with coaching, most learners can master the entire delivery within a week of daily 15-minute sessions.

The remaining steps 1, 3, and 4 are not as tricky, and usually the only mistakes made are omissions. It is important that the coach not neglect any parts of steps 1, 3, and 4. A disregard of anything by the coach will reduce the importance of that point in the learner's mind and will make him or her more apt to abandon its inclusion in his or her training of other workers. Overall, the combination of the JI 10-hour course and a few weeks of kata coaching can produce a very qualified OJT trainer for the organization. An added, and not to be underappreciated, benefit is that anyone proficient as a trainer will understand the JI "pattern" and when being trained on something new, will become an accelerated learner.

The itinerant JI instructor must travel a well-mapped course to achieve an adept level of execution. Using the method ad hoc will not provide the best results. Both of us have found many organizations that have brought us in for the training but claim not to have time for a daily JI Kata. Our retort is usually that a lack of time for improvement is not a reason but rather a problem statement. Taking the training wheels off a bicycle prepares you for the Tour de France no better than taking the JI course and not practicing the kata makes you a good instructor. Practice is the salve for mediocrity.

To create the conditions in which JI Kata can be consistently practiced, a solid JI OJT training program and its associated development of JI-qualified OJT trainers as well as a JI course trainer must be established.

An executive-level manager should be given a budget for the OJT program and take responsibility for the program's success. Management of the program necessarily requires organization-wide coordination of OJT needs. Unit, departmental, and/or sectional training timetables should be constructed and analyzed for percent levels of both interdepartmental and intradepartmental cross-training. Time spent on training should be tracked and analyzed. The amount and frequency of OJT given should also be a measured indicator related to quality and productivity levels. The proliferation and control of Job Instruction breakdowns should be managed with special attention placed on breakdown efficacy. The number of breakdowns isn't as important as their applicability and use. Auditing systems should be organized for ascertaining OJT trainer compliance to all the JI nested Kata.

As described above, the formation and maintenance of a JI OJT program is not trivial. It must, nonetheless, be built in order to create the conditions for appropriately practicing the JI Kata.

3.4 Conclusions

The path is clear:

1. Establish executive-level responsibility and budget;
2. Assemble a well-chosen vanguard of company trainers;
3. Have the TWI-JI course delivered to them;
4. Strategically identify and produce training timetables;
5. Create and review job breakdowns based on efficacy and the training timetables;
6. Supply the correct equipment, tools, and materials for scheduled training;
7. Provide a training regime as close to the actual working conditions as possible for OJT; and
8. Require that trainers support the organization's OJT program with their daily 15-minute practice of the JI Kata.

One should appreciate the facts. The JI course ingeniously provides the development of both the curriculum and the pedagogy your organization needs. The kata instills the pedagogy into your instructor while proper OJT instills the curriculum into the learner. In times of change and uncertainty, Lean cultures are the only kind innovative enough to learn their way through to survival. It would behoove the twenty-first century organization to learn how to teach.

Chapter 4

Coaching Kata: Teaching to Learn

4.1 Introduction

The Coaching Kata is the common thread that runs through the Seven Kata. As each kata is the practice of a specific business-related organizational skill, coaching can assist in propagating these competencies throughout management's ranks. This chapter explains why the development of a Lean Kata culture must begin at the top. It will introduce a coaching philosophy based on process over outcome. We will then present the Coaching Kata as introduced in Toyota Kata. Within the chapter, we have included our experiences revising the Improvement Kata card, closely corresponding to our own coaching journey. The chapter will close with a comprehensive plan for the construction of a kata program that includes the development of coaches.

During our interactions with Mike Rother, he told us on more than one occasion that if things weren't working out in the application of the Improvement Kata, "coaching is the knob you can turn." The Training Within Industry's Job Instruction (TWI-JI) course delivers the same message said differently: "If the worker hasn't learned, the instructor hasn't taught." Both sources place responsibility for proper instruction, training, and coaching on the organization's leaders. This line of reasoning places just as much importance on assessing what the learner understands as it does delivering the instruction/coaching quintessentially. The reader should not dismiss the important skill of teaching, which is just as crucial for Lean transformation as are the skills of improvement and problem solving. Instruction and expert coaching create a foundation for the transmission of a kata.

We then see coaching development as one of the highest priorities in creating a Lean Kata culture. This chapter offers recommendations for developing a standard for coaching within the organization and the formal management of a kata coaching program. Since cultural change requires the acceptance of new paradigms, changes must start in the boardroom. Consequently, we will introduce the notion of the executive as the teacher and defender of the organization's traditions, that is, the *preceptor*.

What follows is the path to coaching proficiency. We feel it important that the reader understand that the Coaching Kata is the most ethereal of the Seven Kata since it cannot be practiced on its own.

4.2 Preceptor Development

During one of our National Institute of Standards and Technology Manufacturing Extension Partnership (NIST MEP)–sponsored staff training events, Conrad once heard an external contracted consultant tell a CEO that "the fish rots from the head down." Anyone involved in a business advisory role understands that a very fine line exists between consult and insult, and it takes a lot of skill to communicate shortcomings without crossing that line. As true as the consultant's statement was to the CEO, it wasn't appreciated.

Within the virtual environment of a book, we can take the liberty of openly agreeing with the consultant's assessment. We have looked long and hard at why Toyota seems so insular and discovered through Liker's book *Toyota under Fire* that the years spent by a Toyota executive learning the proper improvement and problem-solving thinking patterns cannot be easily or quickly taught to managers hired from outside the company.[1]

We believe that for an organization to be successful in building a kata culture that will facilitate the fitting application of Lean's tools, the top decision makers must imprint the kata into their thought processes. If this important step is not taken, other priorities will ultimately interrupt kata activities—something that is lethal to a kata culture. *Daily* is the name of the kata game. In fact, it is our recommendation to all readers; a correct use of the Seven Kata begins with the strategic development of preceptors.

As defined by Webster's Online Dictionary, a preceptor is a teacher responsible to uphold a certain law or tradition, a precept.[2] The Kata preceptor must be a teacher that upholds the Lean tradition. We believe in using non-English words if none in English can definitively express the meaning. We believe the Japanese word *sensei* has been put into that category. We understand that a sensei is a master of a tradition. In our view, *sensei* certainly means more than just teacher, even if teaching is the majority of what a sensei does. We therefore see *preceptor* as a perfectly good English word worthy of rescue from its anachronistic lot.

The preceptor must have a keen understanding of the unique attributes of each of the Seven Kata. The preceptor must also understand their connections to each other and the precepts of Lean. In our experience, we have witnessed far too many of Lean's tools barely understood, marginally used, and eventually discarded into the heap of "things we've tried but didn't work for us." The expeditious development of the organization's preceptor is the imperative that must commence without delay. The chief of operations must be the patron of Lean and therefore must become a preceptor.

The responsibility for the successful conversion from fiat management to a Lean kata culture rests squarely on management's shoulders. If the top two or three are not preceptors, the effort will fail. There are no other answers. Owners, executives, directors all—take heed: you will unconsciously make decisions that defeat Lean without the base of knowledge that only a preceptor can have. Executive-level officers certainly don't have to be the very first preceptors in the organization. They should understand, however, that reluctance in performing a daily kata will delay the cultivation of preceptor perception.

Mastery of the Improvement, Problem Solving (PS), Job Instruction (JI), and Job Relations (JR) Kata are the first steps to the preceptory. The ability to coach them will move the manager toward preceptor status. The Coaching Kata is then the one kata that is used equivalently with all the others. Mastery of any of the other six kata is the prerequisite for coaching that particular kata. Consequently, the coaching of the TWI Kata is the same as the coaching of the *Toyota Kata.*

The TWI-JI course is prescriptive and exact. When attempting to teach a learner a standardized task, there is no better way to train. The pedagogy (four-step method) as well as the curriculum (the task being taught and learned) are presented much like the easily followed icons of a roadmap. The same is true of the Improvement, PS, JR, Job Safety (JS), and Job Methods (JM) Kata. They are all roadmaps to a predetermined destination. This is a major difference from the Coaching Kata.

The Coaching Kata has some prescriptive characteristics, but it is more of a compass than a roadmap. The competent coach keeps the learner on track within the kata confines. Preceptors, however, must also be able to express their reasoned conviction for the method's efficacy. As previously implied, the preceptor is charged with conveying the organization's motives, ideals, and vision. A preceptor then is a very different agent from a coach. Coaching is a skill that is mastered after the coach's own experience as a practitioner has manifested and can somehow be transported into a learner's mind. Precepting is an art that transcends coaching by instilling the spirit of the kata into the learner.

Graduating from coach into a preceptor should become a rewarded career path strategy for all managers operating in a kata culture.

4.3 Coaching Philosophy

We were fortunate enough to have participated in intercollegiate athletics in our youth. As such, we have asked, what coaching characteristics seemed to be the most effective? This is different from asking who our favorite coaches were. An effective coach in the sporting arena is somewhat different from a business coach. The principles are, however, much the same.

Sports may present a decent analog for business, but in no way can sports compare with the volatility that even a small business can experience. In sports, coaches have time between scheduled contests to prepare. In business, this is rarely true. A business cannot stop operations to investigate inadequacies and, if forced to, will usually incur financial losses. This is not to say that a business cannot perform an investigation and take corrective action, but only that it typically is unable to freeze the situation and start over. This is why short, focused, daily improvement activity is the way for a business to improve.

Coincidentally, one of the progenitors of the JI four-step method provides a theoretical framework for the reformation of business coaching as we know it. This forbearer of the JI four-step method is none other than the same Johann Friedrick Herbart we introduced in Chapter 3. He not only developed the pedagogy for modern training methods but is also responsible for making the study of education a science.[3]

Herbart's research included all aspects of education. As is made clear in the JI course, instruction is only a small part of learning.[4] Coaching transcends instruction since genuine concern for the learner should be a coach's primary interest. Coaching is an art, while instruction is a science.

Herbart was the first to advance the notion that education produced a ring of understanding, thus aligning values. Educational philosophers as well as coaches of modern sports all understand a key component of group achievement, that is, an alignment of effort due to similar values.

A wide array of information pertaining to best coaching practices is available at your local bookstore or on the Web. In our opinion, the coaching of sports has evolved a body of knowledge that we feel is relevant. Many coaching philosophies exist, but they are largely values based. Hard work, excellence, and fortitude are common themes, but the alignment of personal values, especially in team sports, transcends attempts at assembling athletes with similar values. A cynical if not commonly asked question is WIFM, or What's in it for me? In a world of individuals with free will, it only makes sense to work to align individuals' values toward a common goal rather than to attempt to change them.

A running coach from Canada by the name of Frank Reynolds had a coaching philosophy that is pertinent to coaching the Lean Kata. Coach Reynolds wrote, "In my opinion, every coaching philosophy should have a major statement on how the coach views the results of both training and competition. I cannot stress enough the importance of educating athletes that it is more important to focus on their process of development and how they performed in competition rather than the results or outcomes that they achieved."[5]

Frank Reynolds passed away in 2008, but his words are as germane within the sports arena as they are to a Lean Kata coach. Just as we have stressed that attention be paid to conditions over metrics in previous chapters, Toyota also pays a high degree of attention to process to achieve more predictable outcomes.[6] We appreciate this sentiment as one deserving careful attention. When coaching, think process before outcome! This point is explained further in Section 4.5.

In the development of your kata coaching philosophy, we suggest consideration of Coach Reynolds's three recommendations:

1. Know yourself, your strengths, your weaknesses, and areas requiring improvement.
2. Know your challenges and the obstacles you'll encounter.
3. Understand the learner, his or her personality, abilities, goals, and why he or she is here.

These three coaching recommendations can go a long way in developing your own coaching philosophy. We will relate these three recommendations to our experiences in coaching the kata.

Recommendation number one reminds us of some of Rother's words in the *Toyota Kata*, "If things aren't working out, coaching is the knob you can turn."[7] Without any cognizance of one's strengths and weaknesses, the coaching "knob" cannot be grasped. Fortunately, facility with JI's nested Kata will provide a standardized assessment tool that can provide for reflection. As anyone who has ever taken the JI course can recite, "If the worker hasn't learned, the instructor hasn't taught."[8]

Luckily for us, countless JI course deliveries combined with hundreds of hours of coaching on-the-job training (OJT) delivery sessions and the breakdown of jobs have made us acutely aware of any single instructional flaw that others or we may make. Our combined 15 years of JI experience and frequent enumerative discussions make us keenly aware of any JI Kata discrepancies encountered. Beyond an appreciation for workforce and systems issues, a comprehensive facility with all Seven Kata, and a contextual understanding of Lean tools, a preceptor must also have a high degree of self-awareness. The JI nested kata provides instructors a template for judging their own proficiency. Recognition of one's own instructional proficiency is certainly the first step to the self-awareness required of coaching.

Reynolds's second recommendation states, "Know your challenges and the obstacles you'll encounter."[9] The greatest obstacle that any organization must first conquer is the development of a preceptor CEO, president, or owner. We have witnessed too many Lean implementations run amok due to upper management decisions made contrary to Lean thinking. Invariably this occurs because decision makers underappreciate considerations necessary for Lean success and base decisions outside of Lean's precepts.

Characteristically, subordinates running an organization will sometimes unconsciously evaluate consistencies in their CEO's thought processes in an attempt to predict acceptable response patterns. It doesn't take long for managers to begin their adoption of Lean precepts after a CEO's Lean decision-making patterns become familiar. All other obstacles beyond the development of an organization's preceptors shrink in comparison.

In the event that some courageous reader decides to use the kata within a limited span of control, we suggest that focus be placed on the perfecting of Improvement Kata activities. Successes with the Improvement Kata might draw positive attention from upper management or other parts of the organization. Recognize that data collection, analysis, and teaming for developing the future-state value stream map is required for the proper targeting of kata activities.

Accomplishing Reynolds's third recommendation depends on a coach's astute insight on the purpose of recommendation number one. A coach must always be alert of where he or she are within the coaching cycle. Only then can a coach afford to fully listen to the learner, not being preoccupied listening to themselves. The kata pattern, regardless of which is being coached, provides a mental map or algorithm that is easily referred back to. Time and effort understanding the learner's inspirations can be focused on if mental energy is not being spent on understanding the kata. A competent coach also understands when to back off and allow the learner latitude as long as the learner is progressing toward the target condition.

We can both attest to the fact that TWI Lead Master Trainer Patrick Graupp's coaching capabilities exceed any techniques coincidentally taught in the JI train-the-trainer course. He has often warned us not to try to copy his style but instead to apply our own personalities to the delivery of any TWI course. In learning to deliver one-on-one OJT or the actual JI course, Patrick's advice is valid. The trainer needs to concentrate his or her efforts on closely following the kata or the scripted trainer's manual, not imitating him. Only after the particular training and/or kata has been internalized can the beginner coach consider applying some of the coaching techniques Patrick availed himself of. Clarity, patience, respect, and kindness are definite traits that will aid in achieving rule number three.

4.4 Coaching

First and foremost, a coach must prepare the learner for any applicable contingency. A coach cannot predict what will happen, only what might happen. In sports, anything within the rules of the game can happen. As such, the coach becomes responsible not only for making sure an athlete's skills are sharp but also for preparing for all foreseeable contingencies. Not understanding this has been one of the greatest limitations of traditional business coaching. For the first time, the Seven Kata provides specific business skills that are as easy to practice as blocking and tackling are in football. The practiced kata become standards for understanding improvement.

The traditional shortcoming of Lean has been what happens between kaizen events. Nothing happens. Lean implementation for many has been a series of punctuated events.

What should be happening is a daily sharpening of managers' improvement or problem-solving skills. The regularity of the kata not only serves as an instrument for skills development and process improvement, but it also provides practice for punctuated team-based events. Everyone on a kaizen team needs to have practiced the same standardized improvement and problem-solving schemes. This provides team members with a common understanding for how to process through improvements or countermeasures to problems.

We're seeing a real demand from top-level managers for ways to self-improve. The methodology adopted must nonetheless be prescriptive, simple, and relevant. The kata are prescriptive in their form, can be flexibly practiced, and are based on operational realities. The kata also provide a common baseline for use during team activities such as kaizen events, quality circles, or task force projects.

A coach should chaperone the learner on their path of discovery. The learner should be allowed to struggle, but not falter. This means letting the learner make small mistakes in the interpretation of any kata elements, but not in the kata course of action. The coach should stop the kata when the mistake has been made and have the learner redo the step correctly. The TWI Kata are previewed in the associated training but are often overlooked by the learner. For kata like the Toyota Kata, which might be introduced to the learner "under fire" without the benefit of previous training, the coach must take care to provide an uncomplicated interpretation of the card and a thorough explanation of any missed points. Regardless, a lessons-learned activity should ensue.

Invariably, in some instances, mistakes will not be readily identifiable. The coach should always provide the learner the benefit of the doubt and keep moving until the mistake is apparent. To be clear, a good coach will let the learner complete the mistake and then provide a complete review. Within that review, the learner should always be asked what the correct action is before it is given. Also, the learner should complete the correction with an opportunity for explanation. Alternatively, when the kata pattern has been violated without the coach's intervention, the coach should take responsibility for the misstep and model a lessons-learned activity.

A kata coaching program is charged with influencing the adaption of a standardized coaching method and providing a developmental path for coaches. A proposed first revision for an Improvement Kata coaching card is presented in Figure 4.1. The card represents the standard coaching method and is an adaption of the one found in *Toyota Kata* under the heading "Guidelines for Deliberate Practice."[10]

All seven steps shown on the card should be completed for every coaching cycle, that is, every 15-minute kata session. Occasionally, a coach should invite a coaching colleague to shadow a coaching cycle and observe if each and every step is addressed during the session. A critique by the shadowing coach should immediately follow the session. Focus can then be placed on any deficits.

Step 1 requires the coach to relate a picture of the whole skill. If the coaching is on TWI Kata, the entire skill has been demonstrated more than one time in the training course. Start the cycle by reminding the learner of the entire skill demonstrated in the course. If, on the other hand, the coaching pertains to one of the Toyota Kata, the coach can have the learner witness the cycle by practicing the kata. Subsequent sessions can begin with a reminder of that kata cycle. In either case, the card can always be pointed to as a representation of the entire skill.

The Five Questions Make Up One Coaching Cycle

1. What is the target condition? (The challenge)

   - What do we expect to be happening?

2. What is the actual condition now?

   - Is the description of the current condition measurable?

   - What did we learn from the last step?

   - Go and see for yourself. Do not rely on reports.

3. What problems or obstacles are now preventing you from reaching the target condition? Which are you addressing now?

   - Observe the process or situation carefully.

   - Focus on one problem or obstacle at a time

   - Avoid Pareto analysis: Do not worry too much about finding the biggest problem right away. If you are moving ahead in fast cycles, you will find it soon.

Rev. 01   4/11

---

4. What is your next step? (Start of next PDCA cycle)

   - Take only one step at a time, but do so in rapid cycles.

   - The next step does not have to be the most beneficial, biggest, or most important. Most important is that you take a step.

   - Many next steps are further analysis, not countermeasures.

   - If next step is more analysis, what do we expect to learn?

   - If next step is a countermeasure, what do we expect to happen?

5. When can we go and see what we have learned from taking that step?

   - As soon as possible. Today is not too soon. How about we go and take that step now? (Strive for rapid cycles!)

Rev. 01   4/11

Figure 4.1   Improvement Kata Card, rev. 01, adapted from *Toyota Kata*.

Step 2 directs the coach to have the learner break the skill into elements (chunking). Our second question to the learner is usually, "So where are we at?" The question evokes a response of event sequence. The learner should then be able to identify which element, in comparison to the coaching cycle that the coach modeled, they are working on. When it is identified, the coach can show the learner what "chunk" they are working on by showing the card.

Step 3 has the learner practice the skill repeatedly in short durations. Repeated focused practice is the gold standard for rapid and complete learning.[11] In step 4, the coach must notice errors and alert the learner to them so that adjustments can be made.

A good coach must pay special attention to step 5. New learners are apt to move quickly through the kata. The coach must slow the process down and have the learner reflect on every step taken.

A wise coach will heed step 6 with mindfulness. If the learner is able to progress through the kata without an error that would derail its direction, the coach can make an edifying comment or two at the end of the session. More may be unnecessary.

The last step is one for the coach to keep in mind. Most people can tell when an individual is motivated. The coach has a responsibility to note a lack of sufficient enthusiasm. If the coach is also a JR Kata coach, they can deal with the issue themselves. If not, they can bring in a preceptor to deal with the situation.

4.5 Coaching and Improvement Kata Card Revision

As a matter of continuous improvement, one should always reflect upon their coaching sessions. Reflection, as defined in *Toyota Kata*, requires the comparison of expected to actual occurrence.[12] The gap between these two—expected and actual—puts into focus what can be reflected upon, enhancing lessons learned. Every coach should perform this kata for every coaching session in which they participate.

We are firm believers in the concept that no organization can copy Toyota by copying Toyota. That is to say, to copy Toyota at its essence would mean not looking to Toyota for answers. Since Toyota develops solutions and improvements for its systems internally, an organization could only copy Toyota by removing their focus from imitation and placing it on introspection.[13]

The Seven Kata teaches the necessary introspective skills for internal improvement. A standard procedure for revising any kata card based on an organization's needs is encouraged. We began our Improvement Kata coaching by copying the Steps for Practical Problem Solving found in *Toyota Kata*.[14] What follows are the reasons the card changed during our first three months of coaching the Improvement Kata.

We began our kata coaching with the PS Kata. As mentioned in both Chapters 2 and 5, a major lesson learned was the practice of due diligence required when observing the same occurrence from many different perspectives. After practicing the coaching for two months with individuals of different skill levels from all shifts on all days, we traveled to Michigan to learn more about the application of the *Toyota Kata* from Mike Rother.

In the training,[15] Mike was clear in communicating that the Improvement Kata was the cultural modifier that simultaneously provides a platform for continuous improvement while building adaptable behavior patterns in managers. He also emphasized the need to perform a value stream analysis to align the Improvement Kata efforts. A recently conducted value stream analysis at an operation willing to conduct the Improvement Kata was a natural fit for initiating Improvement Kata activities.

We initiated activities using revision 1 of the card depicted above in Figure 4.1. This card is copied exactly as found in *Toyota Kata* under the title, "The Five Questions Make Up One Coaching Cycle."[16]

As we used this version, we kept notes on possible revision changes. Conrad recalled Mike explaining why the minimal use of adjectives and adverbs in describing specific target conditions would aid in focusing attention on the state we wish to achieve instead of on metric outcomes alone. Figure 4.2 presents our decision to parenthetically add "(describe without an adjective or adverb)" under the bullet in step 1.

Within three kata sessions that had advanced to step 2, we realized we were going to need more detail for the first bullet. We had inadvertently allowed two learners to progress to step 3 without gathering data. We decided to add the diamond bullets under the first bullet. We didn't feel that the second bullet, "What did we learn from the last step?" was clear. We didn't understand whether that meant step 1 or the collection of data. If it meant step 1, we decided step 3's directive to consider obstacles would send us back to step 1 to redefine a target condition if our initial target condition was too aggressive. If it meant the collection of data, we felt more detail on types of data would be helpful. We decided to eliminate this bullet.

As seen in Figure 4.2, the first item listed in the first diamond became requisite for all kata. We made sure learners drew a block diagram for the initiation of every kata.

The Improvement Kata

FRAMING QUESTIONS

1. What is the target condition? (The challenge)

- What do we expect to be happening,
  (describe without an adjective or adverb)?

2. What is the actual condition now? (Go & See)

- Is the description of the current condition
  measurable?

  ◊ Block diagram, same every cycle?

  ◊ Takt, Cycle times, cycle times vary?

  ◊ Output fluctuation, 1X1 flow, staffing?

  ◊ Capacity/shifts, number of operators?

- Go & See yourself (this is for all of step 2).

3. What obstacles are now keeping you from the target
   condition? Which are you addressing now?

- Observe the process or situation carefully.

- Focus on one problem or obstacle at a
  time. Do not worry about finding the biggest obstacle, just keep cycling fast.

Rev. 02   6/11

THE NEXT EXPERIMENT

4. What is your next step? (Start of next PDCA cycle)

- Take only one step at a time, but do so in
  rapid cycles.

- The next step does not have to be the
  most beneficial, biggest, or most important.
  Most important is that you take a step.

- Many next steps are further analysis, not
  countermeasures.

- If next step is more analysis, what do we
  expect to learn?

- If next step is a countermeasure, what do
  we expect to happen?

PREPARE FOR REFLECTION

5. When can we go and see what we have learned
   from taking that step?

- As soon as possible. Today is not too
  soon. How about we go and take that step
  now? (Strive for rapid cycles!)

15 minutes a day to a better way.

Rev. 02   6/11

Figure 4.2   Improvement Kata Card, rev. 2, adapted from *Toyota Kata*.

The last bullet under step 2, "Go and see yourself. Do not rely on reports" was changed. The directive to not rely on reports seemed obvious because of the combination of going to see and the previously added detailed list of measurable data. Since the go and see is a reminder given as a bullet, we decided to add parenthetically, "(this is for all of step 2)." This statement is commonly used on TWI cards.

In step 3, we decided to combine the last two bullets and eliminated reference to Pareto analysis. We felt that the statement, "Do not worry too much about the biggest problem ..." was redundant after the direction to avoid Pareto analysis. We also thought that many managers in certain sectors may not know what Pareto analysis is, but knew that advising not necessarily picking the biggest problem would be understood by all, so we eliminated reference to Pareto analysis. We underlined "keep cycling fast" to add proper emphasis.

We kept step 4 pretty much intact. The only addition was underlining "rapid cycles" in the first bullet and "take a step" in the second bullet. These were added to bolster what was underlined in step 3 and to emphasize an important aspect of the Improvement Kata, rapid cycling.

As seen in Figure 4.2, the underlining of "(Strive for rapid cycles!)" in the bullet under step 5 was added to coordinate with the previous underlining.

We also decided to add some extra titling, "Framing Questions" for steps 1 through 3, "The Next Experiment" for step 4, and "Prepare for Reflection" for step 5. We added these from information available in *Toyota Kata*.[17]

We also decided to add a hard-to-read slogan at the bottom of the card since we were starting to hand them out to the kata practitioners. The slogan reads, "15 minutes a day to a better way."

The only change to revision 3 depicted in Figure 4.3 is the elimination of the word *problem* from the second bullet in step 3. We definitely wanted to eliminate any reference to the PS Kata and keep the concepts of improvement and problem solving separated. We feel this was a small, but philosophically important, change.

The Improvement Kata

FRAMING QUESTIONS

1. What is the target condition? (The challenge)

 • What do we expect to be happening (describe without an adjective or adverb)?

2. What is the actual condition now?

 • Is the description of the current condition measurable?

 ◊ Block diagram, same every cycle?

 ◊ Takt, Cycle times, cycle times vary?

 ◊ Output fluctuation, 1X1 flow, staffing?

 ◊ Capacity/shifts, number of operators?

 • Go & See yourself (this is for all of step 2)

3. What obstacles are now keeping you from the target condition? Which are you addressing now?

 • Observe the process or situation carefully.

 • Focus on one obstacle at a time. Do not worry about finding the biggest obstacle, keep cycling fast and you'll find it.

Rev. 03   7/11

THE NEXT EXPERIMENT

4. What is your next step? (Start of next PDCA cycle)

 • Take only one step at a time, but do so in rapid cycles.

 • The next step does not have to be the most beneficial, biggest, or most important. Most important is that you take a step.

 • Many next steps are further analysis, not countermeasures.

 • If next step is more analysis, what do we expect to learn?

 • If next step is a countermeasure, what do we expect to happen?

PREPARE FOR REFLECTION

5. When can we go and see what we have learned from taking that step?

 • As soon as possible. Today is not too soon. How about we go and take that step now? (Strive for rapid cycles!)

15 minutes a day to a better way.

Rev. 03   7/11

Figure 4.3 Improvement Kata Card, rev. 3, adapted from *Toyota Kata*.

Figure 4.4 shows the fourth revision of the card. The first change we made was to the first bullet in step 1. In coaching the kata, we realized that we needed to explain the importance of defining *conditions*, so we decided to split off the parenthetical "(describe without an adjective or adverb)" into a second bullet that reads, "List the conditions (w/out adjectives)."

We altered step 2 when we noticed that practitioners were not directly comparing associated items on the list of the target condition to the current state items. We decided to move "Go and see" into parenthesis after "2. What is the actual condition now?" We thought that if it was mentioned on the same line as the actual step, it would be interpreted to be applied to the entire step. We then changed the bullet to "List the actual conditions."

In step 3, we eliminated "Observe the process or situation carefully." We decided that the required *genchi gembutsu* and data collection in step 2 would require the practitioner to observe carefully. We therefore considered the statement somewhat redundant. We replaced it with "Compare current

---

The Improvement Kata

FRAMING QUESTIONS

1. What is the target condition? (The challenge)

   • What do we expect to be happening?

   • List the conditions (w/out adjectives).

2. What is the actual condition now? (Go & See)

   • Is the description of the current condition measurable?

   ◊ Block diagram, same every cycle?

   ◊ Takt, Cycle times, cycle times vary?

   ◊ Output fluctuation, 1X1 flow, staffing?

   ◊ Capacity/shifts, number of operators?

   • List the actual conditions.

3. What obstacles are now keeping you from the target condition? Which are you addressing now?

   • Compare current vs. target conditions.

   • Focus on one obstacle at a time. Do not worry about finding the biggest obstacle, keep cycling fast and you'll find it.

Rev. 04   7/11

THE NEXT EXPERIMENT

4. What is your next step? (Start of next PDCA cycle)

   • Take only one step at a time, but do so in rapid cycles.

   • The next step does not have to be the most beneficial, biggest, or most important. Most important is that you take a step.

   • Many next steps are further analysis, not countermeasures.

   • If next step is more analysis, what do we expect to learn?

   • If next step is a countermeasure, what do we expect to happen?

PREPARE FOR REFLECTION

5. When can we go and see what we have learned from taking that step?

   • As soon as possible. Today is not too soon. How about we go and take that step now? (Strive for rapid cycles!)

15 minutes a day to a better way.

Rev. 04   7/11

Figure 4.4   Improvement Kata Card, rev. 3, adapted from *Toyota Kata.*

vs. target conditions" to make sure the participants were making itemized comparisons of current to target conditions.

4.6 Developing a Kata Culture Using a Training Timetable

As taught in the JI course, a training timetable should be used to keep track of who needs training, on what, and by when. The ranks of ready and able kata coaches should be clearly documented in a similar way. With the number of kata that must be coached, and the specific coaching skills that each coach must master, the coaching training timetable is also valuable for tracking the development of a kata culture.

In Chapter 1 we explained the reasons why achieving the Lean dichotomy of simultaneous change and standardization is so important. The only way to achieve this skill dynamic within the workforce is for the organization to be disciplined in their practices of change and standardization. The organization must achieve a state of constructive change and flexible standardization to successfully apply Lean's tools (see house of Lean). This is why managers must standardize their improvement and standardization skills. What follows is a simplified explanation of the skill-building process for achieving the proper change/standardization balance.

The initial revision of the Coaching Timetable shown in Figure 4.5 depicts the suggested training and kata to be performed by the advance team. In phase 1 a preceptor or Improvement Kata coach should coach each person in the advance team on performing the Improvement Kata. After the initial set of target conditions is met, the advance team should begin TWI Job

		Improvement Kata	Job Instruction Training	
CEO		X	23 - May	
Chief of Staff		X	23 - May	
CFO		X	23 - May	
Controller		X	23 - May	
COO		X	23 - May	
VP, Ops.		X	23 - May	
VP, HR		X	23 - May	
VP, Eng.		X	23 - May	
VP, Sales/Mkt.		X	23 - May	
VP, Cust. Ser.		X	23 - May	

Figure 4.5   Preliminary Coaching Kata Timetable. Example for the Advance Team only.

Instruction training. After the training, a preceptor or JI instructor should begin coaching the advance team on each of the nested kata (see JI Kata, Chapter 3).

In Figure 4.6, we depict the next revision of a Coaching Timetable. In it, part of the advance team begins practicing the JI nested kata within the targeted value stream loops designated for Improvement Kata activity (see Figure 2.1 in Chapter 2). The remainder of the advance team should begin coaching the Improvement Kata with their first set of learners. At the systems level, target conditions for Improvement Kata activity should be prioritized based on pacemaker and value stream loop future state goals. Future state goals should define the vision for the customer. At the operational level, Improvement Kata activity should focus on a process vision for its customer.

In deciding who on the advance team will coach or learn which kata, the preceptor should consider each individual's aptitudes, motivations, and

	Improvement Kata	JI Training	Improvement Coaching	JI 4-Step	JI Breakdown	JR Training	
CEO	X	X	X	5-Oct	30-Sep	5-Dec	
Chief of Staff	X	X	20-Nov	21-Jun	X		
CFO	X	X	20-Nov	21-Jun	5-Jun	5-Dec	
Controller	X	X	X	9-Oct	3-Oct		
COO	X	X	X	8-Oct	4-Oct	5-Dec	
VP, Ops.	X	X	20-Nov	28-Jun	6-Jun		
VP, HR	X	X	X	11-Oct	3-Oct	5-Dec	
VP, Eng.	X	X	20-Nov	1-Jul	7-Jun		
VP, Sales/Mkt.	X	X	20-Nov	8-Jul	8-Jun		
VP, Cust. Ser.	X	X	X			5-Dec	
Dir. Fin. & Acct.	20-Sep		20-Nov				
Dir. Ops.	20-Sep		20-Nov			5-Dec	
Dir. HR	20-Sep		20-Nov			5-Dec	
Dir. Eng.	20-Sep		20-Nov				
Dir. Sales	20-Sep		20-Nov				
Dir. Mkt.	20-Sep		20-Nov				
Dir. Cust. Ser.	20-Sep		20-Nov			5-Dec	
Ops. Mgr.	20-Sep						
HR Mgr.	20-Sep					5-Dec	
Eng. Mgr.	20-Sep						
Mgr. Prod.	20-Nov						
HR Specialist	20-Nov					5-Dec	
Design Eng.	20-Nov						
Process Eng.	20-Nov						
Sales Rep.	20-Nov						
Maint. Spvr.	20-Nov						
Production Lead	20-Nov						
Engineer 1	20-Nov						
Ship. Supv.	20-Nov						
Acct. 2	20-Nov						
QC Tech.	20-Nov						
Office Supv.	20-Nov						

Figure 4.6 Seven Kata Timetable example, expanded (first revision).

predilections. The preceptor should guide the learner toward either learning the nested JI Kata or becoming an Improvement Kata coach. The learning experiences for both groups will be similar but are different. One group of advance team members will learn the Improvement Kata by coaching its standard five-step method to others. The other group of advance team members will learn the JI Kata through its repeated practice.

Each of these two kata is equally important for phase 1 successes. We do realize that the ongoing development of the Coaching Kata is an amelioration of instruction. The JI course and kata provide knowledge and skills applicable to coaching. We believe that some initial coaching experiences before taking the JI course provides valuable context for a better appreciation and broader eventual understanding of JI. To be sure, the Improvement Kata should be learned first, but neither is more important than the other.

Spreading the use of the Improvement Kata throughout management's ranks is therefore the first order of business. Achievements gained by the fast-paced experimenting, learning, and collaboration that managers experience while practicing the Improvement Kata become the self-evident rationale for its continued practice.

Uniquely, the Improvement Kata imprints adaptable behavior patterns into individuals. It provides practitioners immediate beneficial outcomes that encourage the use of this standardized thinking pattern. Increasing each manager's adaptability must be the primary objective when attempting to modify cultural behavior patterns. This point is revisited in the following paragraphs pertaining to rolling out the JR Kata. Suffice it to say, all future kata applications rest on an organization's widespread effective practice of the Improvement Kata.

During the initial round of Improvement and JI Kata activities, a preceptor should monitor the progress of the coaches according to the Coaching Kata.

Figure 4.7 is a representation of a Seven Kata training timetable. As shown, over time, the Improvement Kata represents the baseline skill set that all managers should be able to perform instinctively. The number of qualified JI OJT trainers should be surpassed only by the number of practitioners qualified in the use of the Improvement Kata. Managers, especially in the earlier part of their careers, will need the skill of job instruction gained through the JI Kata. Both improvement and instructional skills are an initial requirement for launching your Lean journey.

4.6.1 JR Connection

As Graupp and Wrona have identified in their book *Implementing TWI*, a clear link between JI and JR exists.[18] So much so, that the authors discuss the decision as to which of these two TWI courses should be offered first. Their conclusion is that it is situational.

Due to cultural dysfunction, the use of the JR Kata may seem to be a necessary step taken before the introduction of JI training. We do agree that dysfunctional relationships hamper improvement efforts. In such situations, their rationale for using JR training before JI is sound. Providing the JR training and including the JR Kata into the "kata mix" would seem to be the logical first step.

The same book describes another connection between the JI and JR courses. It explores the use of JR's four-step method as an approach for helping teams struggling to standardize a task for a JI breakdown. We agree that the JR four-step method should be used for problem resolution involving

	Improvement Kata	JI Training	Improvement Coaching	JI 4-Step	JI Breakdown	JR Training	PS Kata	JR Kata
CEO	X	X	X	5-Oct	30-Sep	5-Dec		30-Jan
Chief of Staff	X	X	20-Nov	X	X			
CFO	X	X	20-Nov	X	X	5-Dec		30-Jan
Controller	X	X	X	9-Oct	3-Oct			
COO	X	X	X	8-Oct	4-Oct	5-Dec		30-Jan
VP, Ops.	X	X	20-Nov	X	X			
VP, HR	X	X	X	11-Oct	3-Oct	5-Dec	15-Feb	
VP, Eng.	X	X	20-Nov	X	X			
VP, Sales/Mkt.	X	X	20-Nov	X	X			
VP, Cust. Ser.	X	X	X			5-Dec	12-Feb	
Dir. Fin. & Acct.	X		20-Nov					
Dir. Ops.	X		20-Nov			5-Dec		
Dir. HR	X		20-Nov			5-Dec	7-Feb	
Dir. Eng.	X		20-Nov					
Dir. Sales	X		20-Nov					
Dir. Mkt.	X		20-Nov					
Dir. Cust. Ser.	X		20-Nov			5-Dec	10-Feb	
Ops. Mgr.	X							
HR Mgr.	X					5-Dec	8-Feb	
Eng. Mgr.	X							
Mgr. Prod.	20-Nov							
HR Specialist	20-Nov					5-Dec	6-Feb	
Design Eng.	20-Nov							
Process Eng.	20-Nov							
Sales Rep.	20-Nov							
Maint. Spvr.	20-Nov							
Production Lead	20-Nov							
Engineer 1	20-Nov							
Ship. Supv.	20-Nov							
Acct. 2	20-Nov							
QC Tech.	20-Nov							
Office Supv.	20-Nov							

Figure 4.7 Seven Kata Training Timetable, expanded with PS Kata & JR Kata.

people. We, however, view the JR course's more proactive Foundations for Good Relations as socially valuable. These are learnable considerations that will enhance coaching.

As will be explained in Chapter 6, the *foundations*, as we refer to them, are not a part of the JR Kata. Even though they are presented as a key factor of the JR course, they do not provide a predictable pattern of practice, one requirement of a kata. JR's foundations do however enhance the Coaching Kata with a mental model for replicating a business coach's countenance. Since the foundations are preventive medicine, we recommend their consideration as a key element to coaching. This is another reason that we consider the JR Kata the cultural fortifier.

Because of Conrad's recent research confirming Rother's findings, we are of like mind in agreeing that the practice of the Improvement Kata is the cultural modifier that quickly builds adaptable behavior patterns within management's ranks.[19] We therefore conclude that the delivery and practice of the JR training and kata during or prior to Improvement and JI Kata activities can become overwhelming and is probably unnecessary.

Figures 4.5, 4.6, and 4.7 all depict an initial JR training scheduled for upper management and the human resources department. It is scheduled some six months after upper management's initiating their first kata activities. The schedule is idealized, and your organization should make adjustments based on needs. The initial JR training should be kept on the coaching timetable as a visible approaching eventuality. It can also be considered a mark of kata program maturity. A perceived need for a leadership-based kata will eventually surface, and when it does, the JR training and kata activity should begin, albeit at a measured pace.

The Improvement Kata compels organizational collaboration, which serves as a springboard from which the skill of job relations (JR Kata) can be launched. A preceptor understands that the JR Kata is one of three problem solving kata, the first of which managers should learn. Even though the JR Kata focuses on developing a standard skill for dealing with relational difficulties, it is frequently a manager's first experience in standardized problem solving. The JR Kata significance is in how it cultivates the adroit use of all Seven Kata by correlating improvement and problem solving with human relations.

As shown in Figure 4.8, the remaining three coaching kata categories (PS, JS, and JM) on the training timetable have fewer coaches than the other three kata. These three kata are used in various ways and to different degrees given the circumstances and needs of the organization.

	Improvement Kata	JI Training	Improvement Coaching	JI 4-Step	JI Breakdown	JR Training	JR Kata	PS Kata	
CEO	X	X	X	X	X	5-Dec		30-Jan	
Chief of Staff	X	X	X	X	X				
CFO	X	X	X	X	X	5-Dec		30-Jan	
Controller	X	X	X	X	X				
COO	X	X	X	X	X	5-Dec		30-Jan	
VP, Ops.	X	X	X	X	X			30-Jan	
VP, HR	X	X	X	X	X	5-Dec	15-Feb		
VP, Eng.	X	X	X	X	X				
VP, Sales/Mkt.	X	X	X	X	X				
VP, Cust. Ser.	X	X	X			5-Dec	12-Feb		
Dir. Fin. & Acct.	X	X							
Dir. Ops.	X		X			5-Dec			
Dir. HR	X		X			5-Dec	7-Feb		
Dir. Eng.	X		X						
Dir. Sales	X		X						
Dir. Mkt.	X		X						
Dir. Cust. Ser.	X		X			5-Dec	10-Feb		
Ops. Mgr.	X								
HR Mgr.	X					5-Dec	8-Feb		
Eng. Mgr.	X								
Mgr. Prod.	X								
HR Specialist	X					5-Dec	6-Feb		
Eng. Mgr/Prod.	X								
Eng. Mgr. Des.	X								
Sales Mgr.	X								
Maint. Supv.	X								
Production Lead	X								
Prod. Supv.	X								
Ship. Supv.	X								
Acct. Rec. Supv.	X								
Quality Supv.	X								
Office Supv.	X								
Quality Mgr.	Feb-29								
Security Supv.	Feb-29								
Payroll Supv.	Feb-29								

Figure 4.8   Example of suggested Training Timetable for the Seven Kata.

Just as the JI Kata supports the Improvement Kata in the first phase of kata culture development, in the second phase, the JI and JR Kata support the practice of the PS Kata.

4.6.2 Coaching the Problem-Solving Kata

Special attention should be paid to the PS Kata. Optimally, skill in the JR kata would precede the learning of the PS Kata. We discovered that during the PS Kata cause investigation, more often than not, a human task would surface within the causal chain of events. In such circumstances, facility with the JR Kata is a great advantage.

Depending on the organization's circumstances, the PS Kata skill might need to be learned and practiced all the way to the team lead level, but generally, the PS Kata should be a skill required of all candidates for management positions with budget authority. In practicing the PS Kata, it was noted that change authorization became protracted due to the scope of change required. Unlike the quick experimental process exhibited by the Improvement Kata, larger resource requirements and changes in practices are often recommended as countermeasures to problems dealt with by the PS Kata. This is why we recommend all managers attain the PS Kata skill by the time they are given budget authority.

Another characteristic of those coaching the PS Kata is that they are commonly preceptors, although a JR Kata coach could begin coaching the PS Kata before attaining preceptor status. Either a preceptor can coach the JS and JM Kata, or if the organization is large enough, a qualified individual specified for that purpose could coach these kata. Examples may include an engineer or Six Sigma black belt that coaches the JM Kata or a Safety Committee member coaching the JS Kata.

Phase 1, as described above, includes the widespread exercise of both the Improvement and JI Kata; they will take a while to promulgate. The correct performance of these two kata is not trivial and takes time and effort to perfect. Adherence to the 15-minute daily rule can bring amazing results within an 18-month to two-year timeframe. When the workforce experiences the Improvement Kata effect and begins receiving its cultural benefits, the focus on a broader coaching development program and consideration of when and how to leverage the other kata can ensue.

The Coaching Training Timetable is a comprehensive tool that also facilitates a visual impression of your Lean Kata culture's developmental process. The Coaching Kata card used at the tactical level in combination with the strategic understanding provided by use of the training timetable is your key to awakening the life forces in your Lean management system.

4.7 Conclusion

As described in this chapter, a manager must steadily matriculate from possibly coaching the Improvement Kata at a rudimentary level, to becoming a proficient OJT trainer, to coaching multiple kata, to potentially the achievement of preceptor status. The main point of this chapter concerns facilitation and development of a kata culture. Hopefully, the reader understands that Improvement Kata success is the priority, and the other kata are brought on in support of it.

Chapter 5

Problem-Solving Kata: Seek to Understand Kata

When forces gather that work to undermine current standards, the Problem-Solving (PS) Kata is a fundamental tool that should be applied to maintain the norm. We then place the PS Kata into the maintenance kaizen category.

5.1 Unconsciously Neglecting Problems

The PS Kata is a powerful method for engaging management in the act of problem resolution. The caveat however is that many people actually prefer off-the-cuff conversations, debates, and even commiseration above the regimented thinking required for effective problem resolution. Poorly conducted workplace meetings are more about talking and airing opinions than about actually solving the problem at hand. The PS Kata is the quintessential action for an organization to take, but only when management realizes that their unproductive meeting-oriented culture will never be able to keep up with the complexity and quantity of problems all organizations face.

If an organization's managers are forever solving the same issue, or worse yet, spending months or years working on a single concern, chances are the organization is unconsciously neglecting their deep-rooted problems. The poor practice of ad hoc problem solving in "seat of the pants" meetings and conversely the rigor and discipline necessary for the proper application of the PS Kata are examined further. A simple analogy might be the general issue of diet and exercise.

Question: Why do many people overeat, and eat the wrong things?
Answer: Because it's comfortable.
Question: Why don't people exercise more frequently and intensively?
Answer: Because it's uncomfortable.

Meetings and the PS Kata are the diet and exercise of the organization. If an individual eats more frequently with less volume (i.e., balanced choices, lower calories) and consistently exercises, they will produce a leaner, more capable body. Likewise, if an organization meets more frequently with less volume (i.e., shorter duration, more focus) and consistently uses the PS Kata, they will produce a leaner, more capable organization. We all know what to do, but in either case, it takes self-mastery to institute and continue the behavior.

This initial objective must be internalized or else the discipline necessary to use the kata will evaporate. If management acknowledges their problem-solving deficit (no small feat), the next objective is to find a kata coach for managers. We highly recommend that a preceptor (see Chapter 4) perform the coaching of the PS Kata since this kata is directly targeted at management and can have negative consequences if performed inadequately.

The PS Kata, constantly practiced, satisfies dual purposes. First, it solves problems even at the most granular level. It also conditions the practitioner to accept any newly found solution. This is accomplished by using the identified problem as a vehicle for teaching this special problem-solving technique. Using the technique repetitively will make both the learner and the system more adaptive.

The system in general and other managers specifically are more adaptable to solutions vetted by the PS Kata if they themselves are practitioners of the PS Kata. Time wasted in meetings and discussions is saved because other managers, skilled at the PS Kata, understand that the problem was approached from all conceivable angles and that a number of solutions were attempted. Most of all, they understand that due diligence was performed. They know that the solution was not a guess or someone's off-the-cuff good idea.

5.2 PS Kata

So what is this "special" problem-solving technique? It is indeed special, but not unfamiliar. It is simply Shewhart's plan–do–check–act (PDCA) problem-solving cycle, albeit with a couple of additions.[1] The Toyota PS Kata shown in Figure 5.1 also includes "Grasping the situation" prior to the application

STEPS FOR PRACTICAL PROBLEM SOLVING	5 QUESTIONS-COACHING CYCLE

1. Pick Up the Problem: Problem Consciousness
    Identify the problem that is a priority.
 	
2. What is the actual condition now? (Go & See)
• Is the description of the current condition
  measurable?
    • What should be happening?
    • What is actually happening?
    • Break the problem into individual problems if necessary
• If necessary use temporary measure to contain the abnormal
  occurrence until the root cause can be addressed
• Locate the point of cause of the problem
    Do not go into cause investigation until you find the point
    of cause.
• Grasp the tendency of the abnormal occurrence at the point of
  cause
 	
3. Investigate Causes
• Identify and confirm the direct cause of the abnormal
  occurrence
• Conduct a 5 – Why investigation to build a chain of
  cause/effect relationships to root cause.
• Stop at the cause that must be addressed to prevent
  recurrence.
 	
4. Develop and Test Countermeasures
• Take one specific action to address the root cause
• Try to change only one factor at a time so you can see
  correlation
 	
5. Follow Up
• Monitor
• Standardize successful countermeasures
  correlation
• Reflect, what did we learn during this problem solving
  process?
	Framing Questions
	
	    1. What is the target condition (the challenge)?
	
	    2. What is the actual condition now?
	
	    3. What obstacles are now preventing you from
	       reaching the target condition?
	
	       Which one are you addressing now?
	
	The Next Experiment
	
	    4. What is your next step? (start of next PDCA
	       cycle / experiment)
	
	Prepare for Reflection
	
	    5. When can we go and see what we have
	       learned from taking that step?

Figure 5.1   Toyota Kata.

of PDCA and "Reflection" subsequent to it. The PS Kata requirement of "Grasping the situation" is a defining deference between the PS Kata and the Improvement Kata. These additions are like a map and rudder, both used in navigating a vessel to "true north."[2]

Unlike the Improvement Kata that should be used in conjunction with a value stream analysis, the PS Kata can be applied independently whenever the need arises. As a part of maintenance kaizen, problem solving should be both immediate as well as appropriate. The level of immediacy can take the 15-minute kata time limit off the table. In such cases, the PS Kata must instantaneously transform from a kata used primarily for skill development, to a just-in-time application that swiftly ameliorates the organization's latest predicament. Just as in martial arts, a kata is for training and conditioning and is not necessarily used completely in actual combat. It is important, nonetheless, that the PS practitioner have experienced extensive practice of the PS Kata in preparation for "combat conditions."

The broad use of the Improvement Kata requires multiple alignment factors since the probability of contradictory improvements increases with the increased number of managers using it. Aside from value stream analysis as an aligning factor, recall that the target condition for Improvement Kata performed on the same process step must be the same. This requirement is another aligning factor evident at an even more granular level than the value stream. None of these types of alignment factors are necessary for the PS Kata because problem solving, if performed correctly, is a one-up event.

The PS Kata (see Figure 5.1) is a five-step process. The following will describe the PS Kata as coached, detailing each of the steps.

Step 1. Pick Up the Problem: Problem Consciousness
  − Identify the problem that is a priority.

Step 1 is brief but important to fully consider. The bullet directs attention to prioritization. This is a first-glance conception of the problem. Unlike many of the steps that follow, step 1 will focus on a more magnified view of the problem. Prioritization requires a more global perspective. The PS Kata provides a mechanism of weighted importance to the learner before proceeding to more detailed scrutiny.

Step 2. Grasp the Situation (Go and See)

Go and see is for the whole of step 2 and implies how one is actually supposed to grasp the situation.

Going to see also facilitates kaizen teian activity. *Kaizen teian* is the Japanese-style workforce proposal system and is very different from traditional American suggestion systems. One of the basic tenets of the teian system that must also be practiced when performing the Improvement Kata is for managers to become "walking suggestion boxes."[3] The point of teian is to get managers out into the workplace (i.e., gemba) to observe the work and engage the workforce on possible improvements. The go and see required by the PS Kata means collecting not only visual information but also any available verbal or tabulated data. The workforce is always a rich source of relevant information, and asking a worker for a proposal on an idea that surfaced during the manager's PS Kata investigation not only will assist in this instance of maintenance kaizen, but it is also an excellent means of promoting worker buy-in for improvement kaizen.

As the PS Kata is practiced, the learner comes to realize that even the most earnest application of PDCA is not enough. A problem must first be precisely defined to suitably grasp the situation. As the famous twentieth century American engineer Charles Kettering stated, "A problem well stated is a problem half solved."[4] The problem statement becomes the target locator for application of PDCA.

The practitioner's first attempt at a problem statement, regardless of focus and articulation, is frequently not the problem that will eventually be resolved. The reason is that based on both process analysis and root cause analysis, in almost all cases, more nuances to a seemingly simple problem will be revealed. These fine distinctions must then be dealt with individually, thus changing the focus of the problem statement.

The PS Kata provides the process interrogation tools needed for problem solving. Notice how each of the following bullet points will add another level of scrutiny to the problem statement. This closer examination provides a deeper and more contextual appreciation of the problem's intricacies.

- Clarify the problem.

In attempting to clarify a problem, the learner must pare the problem concept down into an easily understood sentence. Putting thoughts to paper has a focusing effect. This practice begins a process that keeps the problem analysis on track and away from tangential issues.

- What should be happening?
- What is actually happening?

These two bullet points work synergistically to define the performance gap. This bounding measure helps confine the problem and places perspective on it. Notice that this step is identical to the starting point in the Improvement Kata.

- Break the problem into individual problems if necessary.

Disaggregating the problem evokes a different perception of it. Even when a problem is thought to be well defined, using step 2 can actually produce the consequence of having to return to step 1 to redefine a narrower part of the problem.

If, per chance, the practitioner has at least taken the Training Within Industry (TWI) Job Methods (JM) course, the problem sequence may be subject to the 5W1H, ECRS (what, why, where, when, who, how or how much; eliminate, combine, rearrange, simplify) used by Kipling's JM Kata (see Chapter 8). The analysis can result in waste elimination and the reconfiguration of the problem's associated process. Process streamlining, when warranted, can generate unanticipated valuable improvements disguised as countermeasures. This path, however, can only be pursued with a PS Kata practitioner knowledgeable in the JM process. The use of JM, primarily an improvement kaizen tool, can serve a further purpose when occasionally applied to maintenance kaizen problem solving.

- If necessary, use a temporary measure to contain the abnormal occurrence until the root cause can be addressed.

This bullet point reminds the practitioner that defect containment should be considered before moving on to the development of a permanent countermeasure. In an example such as a production environment, this is an especially important factor since unplanned downtime can translate to appreciable monetary losses.

- Locate the point of cause of the problem. Do not go into cause investigation until you find the point of cause.

This point requires the practitioner to make a first attempt at looking for the root of the problem. The word *locate* is used for a reason. The learner should be reminded that going to see still pertains to this part of step 2 and occurs in a physical location, that is, gemba. The second sentence is also a reminder of restraint, patience, and the full consideration of alternative candidates for the root cause.

- Grasp the tendency of the abnormal occurrence at the point of cause.

This bullet point requires a temporal focus, specifically the frequency of the occurrence. Knowing how often something happens can change one's perception of the true magnitude of the problem. In a data-rich environment, it may be possible to obtain numbers that reveal measures of central tendency and variation. Such statistics are a valuable form of information that can enhance understanding. The use of statistical methods, however, is beyond the scope of this book.

Step 3. Investigate Causes
   – Identify and confirm the direct cause of the abnormal occurrence.

This first bullet point requires the consideration of possible precursors to the emergence of the undesirable event at the initial point of cause. The PS Kata is specifically inducing reconsideration of the possibility of a deeper core cause.

   – Conduct a 5-Why investigation to build a chain of cause-and-effect relationships to the root cause.
   – Stop at the cause that must be addressed to prevent recurrence.

After having considered three different times what the root cause is, the goal of these two bullet points is to direct the learner to develop a chain of events. This 5-Why process starts at the original question, "What is currently happening" (step 2, "Clarify the problem"), and cascades down to what the practitioner has assessed as the root cause. Occasionally it is impossible to eliminate the root cause. In spite of this, when this chain of events is fully developed, a link in the chain can be removed. Breaking a link prevents a source event, which can avert the problem.

Step 4. Develop and Test Countermeasures
   – Take one specific action to address the root cause.
   – Try to change only one factor at a time so you can see correlation.

The phrasing "develop and test" is a euphemism for *experiment*. The PDCA cycle is used to conduct as many experiments as needed to solve the problem. The bullets in step 4 are reminders to keep the experiments simple. The student is directed to hold everything constant and use only one test variable at a time during any single experiment.

Step 4 should be second nature for a learner who has learned the Improvement Kata. The PDCA cycles should be conducted identically to step 4 in the Improvement Kata. In fact, the use of Rother's PDCA cycle sheet[5] at this point of the PS Kata is encouraged and closely follows steps 4 and 5 for both the Improvement and PS Kata.

Step 5. Follow Up
  – Monitor and confirm results.

This bullet point directs the practitioner to scrutinize the experiment while in progress to detect any anomalies. It also suggests that more than one experiment be conducted to substantiate the original experimental results.

  – Standardize successful countermeasure.

The learner is directed to make sure the countermeasure is practiced and sustained thereafter. The uses of TWI Job Instruction, visual controls, and error proofing are methods that can accomplish the establishment of a new standard. The learner's knowledge of TWI-JI and 5S (Sort, Set-In-Order, Shine, Standardize, Sustain) can be of benefit in his or her efforts to standardize the countermeasure.

Again, this is another occurrence of the need for the organization to have adopted JI Kata practices.

  – Reflect: What did we learn during the problem-solving process?

After observing, questioning, and analyzing the problem, unanticipated perspectives become apparent. This new awareness should be examined.

As shown, the PS Kata is a predefined form or pattern for problem solving. It also can be learned and passed on to others. In an organization, it is of paramount importance that it be taught and learned within the ranks of management if a continual improvements culture is the strategic objective. As mentioned above, outcomes should be predicted for comparison with actual outcomes. The comparison of expected to actual outcomes is a learning experience and helps to focus reflection.

5.3 PS Kata Family

A similar, if not identical, problem-solving course is formally taught at Toyota. Toyota's Practical Problem Solving training was at one time a mainstay in Toyota's training regimen. Toyota Business Practices (TBP) is the current manifestation of the same problem-solving process with the added benefit of depicting the eight-step TBP/PDCA relationship.[6] The PS Kata title as shown in the *Toyota Kata* is a conspicuous "Steps for Practical Problem Solving."[7] The relationship between TBP and the PS Kata is apparent. As

Steps for Practical Problem Solving	TBP 8 Steps

1. Pick Up the Problem: Problem Consciousness
• Identify the problem that is a priority
2. Grasp the situation (Go and See)
• Clarify the problem.
    • What should be happening?
    • What is actually happening?
    • Break the problem into individual
      problems if necessary
• If necessary use temporary measure to contain
  the abnormal occurrence until the root cause
  can be addressed.
• Locate the point of cause of the problem. Do
  not go into cause investigation until you find
  the point of cause.
• Grasp the tendency of the abnormal occurrence
  at the point of cause.
3. Investigate Causes
• Identify and confirm the direct cause of the
  abnormal occurrence.
• Conduct a 5-Why investigation to build a chain
  of cause/effect relationships to root cause.
• Stop at the cause that must be addressed to
  prevent recurrence.
4. Develop and Test Countermeasures
• Take one specific action to address the root
  cause.
• Try to change only one factor at a time, so that
  you can see correlation.
5. Follow Up
• Monitor and confirm results.
• Standardize successful countermeasure.
• Reflect. What did we learn during the problem -
	PLAN
	1. Define the problem relative to the ideal.
	2. Break down the problem into manageable
	    pieces.
	3. Identify the root cause.
	4. Develop alternate solutions.
	5. Evaluate and select the best solution based on
	    what is known.
	DO
	6. Implement the solution (on a trial basis if
	    possible).
	CHECK
	7. Check the impact of the solution.
	ACT
	8. Adjust, standardize, and spread based on what
	    has been learned.

Figure 5.2   Comparison of the PS Kata steps and the Toyota Business Practice Steps.

shown in Figure 5.2, the PS Kata is much more detailed than the eight steps of TBP. As Shakespeare wrote, "A rose by any other name is still a rose."

Another documented version of a similar Toyota practice is kaizen circle activity (KCA).[8] A difference is that KCA isn't specifically focused on an individual's problem-solving skill but rather is a team-oriented process for improvement, much like a quality circle.[9] A similarity between KCA and the PS Kata is the learn-by-doing approach used by both. As mentioned in the opening passages of Chapter 2, problem solving is an integral part of maintenance kaizen. TBP and the PS Kata are about an individual working to maintain the stability of a process with the ultimate goal of eliminating abnormal occurrences. KCA uses its version of the similar problem-solving process used by both TBP and the PS Kata, but instead employs it in a team setting. A KCA team should be well practiced in the PS Kata to avoid dis-agreements on process and place focus on content.

We have now seen situations where improvement kaizen skills such as the JM Kata can lend their application to maintenance kaizen, and also the reverse, where in certain circumstances, TBP and the PS Kata skills (or parts of them) can be applied to improvement kaizen efforts. The JI Kata also surfaces as a required skill in both improvement and maintenance kaizen situations. The ability of a manager to bring out the right combination of any of the skills taught by the Seven Kata, given the situation at hand, translates to the high levels of organizational performance required by Lean—again, skills, not tools!

It may have seemed that the PS Kata, TBP, and KCA are all a disjointed jumble of kaizen approaches. Actually, any given Toyota plant's maturity level indicates how many cycles of learning have been instilled into that plant's culture. By virtue of this level of maturity, a new U.S.-based plant's personnel cannot be expected to be in the same place on the learning curve that, say, a 50-year-old Japanese Toyota plant is.[10]

5.4 Training within Industry Problem-Solving Training

The TWI-PS[11] course was developed in the 1950s in the United States. Unlike the other four TWI courses that run 10 hours, the PS course is 40 hours in duration. The first 10 hours is designed much like the other three TWI 10-hour courses. The next 20 hours is allotted to participants, who then apply the method on a problem identified in their workplace. The last 10 hours consists of a group report for results and lessons learned from the application of the method.

The pedagogy of the TWI-PS course is like the PS Kata in that the learn-by-doing approach is applied. TWI-PS follows a four-step method for problem resolution:

1. Isolate the problem.
2. Prepare for solution.
3. Correct the problem.
4. Check and evaluate results.

This sequence also follows the PDCA cycle. Steps 1 and 2 include the planning phase. Step 3 is the doing phase, and step 4 is the checking phase. The practitioner can then make an informed decision for the act/adjust phase of PDCA. Analysis of each part of the TWI-PS four-step method corresponds closely to the PS Kata as well as the TBP course. TWI-PS, however, is set up to have the participant identify problems that are resolved using one or a combination of the methods taught in the other four 10-hour TWI courses.

To decide which of the four courses to use for the identified problem's countermeasure, the problem is characterized as one of Ishikawa's 4Ms (materials, machines, methods, manpower).[12] A root cause based on materials or machines may be able to be resolved by one or more of the four 10-hour TWI courses, depending on the situation. Problems incurred by poor job methods are typically resolved with either the JM or JI courses or both. Manpower-based problems are typically resolved with either the JR or JI courses or both.

With people-based problems, four possible personal situations are posed pertaining to the person or people:

- Don't know
- Can't do
- Don't care
- Won't do

These four personal circumstances lead to three possibilities; the person or people either were given or have:

- Faulty instruction
- Wrong assignment
- Personality situation

As with both TBP's and KCA's close connection to the PS Kata, the TWI-PS course overlaps with the PS Kata at many different levels. If the kata student has facility with any of the TWI courses, including TWI-PS, the practice of the PS Kata is enhanced.

5.5 Six Sigma in Context

We recognize Six Sigma as a skill set apart from those required by Lean. It is our opinion that every manager within the organization can, at some level, learn the seven Lean skills identified in this book. This is often not true of Six Sigma. As part of our experience, we've seen organizations expend appreciable resources training a wide swath of management at the green belt level only to have them forget concepts from a lack of application. On the other hand, we have witnessed the broad use of the Lean skills learned through the kata as a catalyst for daily incremental improvement, a concept apart from most organizations practicing Six Sigma.

Organizations that practice Six Sigma exclusively are often unable to sustain their results, especially where human interactive processes are concerned. We've had the opportunity to work with organizations that provide their engineers and managers with Lean Six Sigma training. It is our opinion that the moniker Lean Six Sigma is definitely correct in its sequential arrangement. The typical Lean Six Sigma training, however, begins and ends with the rigorous treatment of statistical techniques at the expense of little to no study of Lean's true implication, that of workforce development.

Our understanding of these tools indicates that the prolific use of Six Sigma prior to the full development of a kata culture is premature. Both the PS and Improvement Kata provide ample opportunity to introduce the collection and analysis of data. Statistical methods have their place, but deft application of these powerful tools is more often than not missing. Six Sigma is introduced in this chapter because of its obvious use in problem solving. These tools, nonetheless, can be applied in varying degrees within the other kata.

A day will come when an organization steeped in a Seven Kata culture would take Six Sigma application to a new level. A mature kata culture would imply that much of the low-hanging "qualitative" fruit had been picked, and that quantitative tools with ever-higher levels of resolution become necessary. Six Sigma tools may also have a tightly defined relevance in highly technical occupations, but by and large, many of Six Sigma's tools are overkill for most managers.

We must always consider one of Einstein's bromides to the lesser of his species: "Everything can be counted, but not everything counts."[13]

5.6 Conclusions

Conrad had the occasion to practice the PS Kata before learning the Improvement Kata. We have suggested that the PS Kata be taught to managers who at least have had the opportunity to learn the Improvement Kata first. We have several reasons for this advice.

Recall from Chapter 2 that PDCA cycling should be as accelerated as possible. We said that choosing the largest or most important obstacles to work on isn't as important as cycling experiments quickly because the practitioner will get to them soon enough. Rapid PDCA cycling provides the benefits of constant insightful learning, a sense of progress, and optimistic experimentation.

The Improvement Kata starts by defining a gap in performance and focuses efforts on improving. The PS Kata starts by defining the problem and focuses efforts on eliminating the threat. Some might find Taoist qualities in the two-kata relationship. It is, nonetheless, our opinion that the positive energy created on improving is an important constructive dynamic in the development of a Lean culture. The Improvement Kata provides many levels of support for the cultural transformation process. Learning, awareness, strategy, and technique are all taught by the Improvement Kata.

The PS Kata is a powerful tool that every organization should have robust capability in. It is, however, a skill that can be easily misapplied. Fault is one logical step removed from cause, and cause is an important feature of problem solving. As a matter of practicality, if the cause of a problem is human behavior and the behavior is beyond the practitioner's span of authority, human relations and the chain of command can present a dicey situation. Problem solving should be encouraged and taught to those who can affect the solution and have excellent relationship skills.

In the best of situations, a PS Kata practitioner will have had experience not only with the Improvement Kata but also with the JR Kata. Chapter 6 describes the relationship between the PS and JR Kata. Suffice it to say, the practice of the PS Kata may require "political" acumen, which is best learned before attempting to change others' practices.

Conrad did identify one advantage of practicing the PS Kata first. In having to proceed through the protracted and lengthy problem-solving process, Conrad thought that the contemplation needed for the proper application of the Improvement Kata was exemplified. This is in accordance with the Lean paradox, "You must learn to go slow to go be able to go fast."[14,15]

The PS Kata is a comprehensive standardized process for ensuring the performance and acceptance of maintenance kaizen. In this chapter, we identified one possible point within the kata where statistical techniques could play an important role, but warned of the misuse of Six Sigma tools. We also identified in TWI-PS a noteworthy method for dealing with all aspects of human performance. Using a panoply of problem-solving techniques without an underlying guiding precept leads to confusion and problem-solving orthodoxies that are not conducive to creativity. The proper tools, used properly, as opposed to choosing the tool that we know, is the moral of the PS story. The Seven Kata are the holistic set of qualitative skills crucial for managing a Lean culture. The PS Kata is an imperative for maintenance kaizen.

Chapter 6

Job Relations Kata: The Cultural Fortifier

The repetitive practice of a slightly altered Job Relations (JR) four-step method is what we refer to throughout this book as the JR Kata. Our goal for this chapter is to leave the reader with an understanding of how the JR Kata supports the other six kata, when and how it should be introduced, and how the coaching and practice of the kata should be conducted.

6.1 Collaboration and Conciliation

In Chapter 1, we depict the Improvement Kata as Lean's cultural modifier. That chapter explained how collaboration propagates through goal setting, shared experimentation, and learning. Improvement Kata activity also fosters empathy for those whose work efforts are thwarted by system dysfunction. This additional feature of the Improvement Kata will usually catch the fledgling practitioner off guard. Given time, Improvement Kata activity provides a sense of *esprit de corps* to those practicing it. This camaraderie is an important feature of the cultural modification referred to.

As mentioned, collaboration is typically an eye-opener to those new to the Improvement Kata. Since the Improvement Kata is initially perceived solely as a way to improve processes, most new to the Improvement Kata are surprised upon the revelation that it also facilitates better communication and cooperation—the crucible of improvement. This dynamic is completely different from that of the JR Kata.

Our contention is that the positive nature of collaboration is the qualifying precondition for the development of a Lean Kata culture. The Training Within Industry (TWI) JR training and subsequent practice of the JR Kata provide the learner with a standard way of dealing with the complexity of human relations, something that the Improvement Kata doesn't necessarily offer. If then the Improvement Kata is the cultural modifier, we might consider the JR Kata the cultural fortifier. This is not meant to imply that the use of the Improvement and JR Kata will wipe away all human contention within an organization. The two kata can, nevertheless, provide the cultural environment in which a Lean transformation can flourish.

The TWI-JR course provides a well-vetted problem-solving method that focuses specifically on human relations. Those experiencing human relations difficulties within their ranks often request that the TWI-JR training course be given first. A perceived need to familiarize employees with the tenets of civility will usually induce management to seek out training that focuses on leadership and/or interpersonal relations. As we have explained in the previous chapters, the key to behavior modification is the focused repeated practice of a form or pattern by a learner.

Typical relationship training seeks to inform participants on the behaviors that the organization finds acceptable. Such training may even include instruction on dealing with interrelational problems that do arise. Rarely though does relationship training require the ongoing practice of a standard method upon the training's culmination. Awareness training alone is of limited value. Fortunately, the JR Kata provides learners with a repeatable algorithm that attends to the human difficulties that will invariably arise. The JR Kata then is clearly a form of maintenance kaizen. Problem solving is, after all, an attempt to maintain the status quo. The JR Kata problem-solving nature and its inherent investigative process drives conciliation, not collaboration—two very different dynamics.

6.2 Practicing the JR Kata

The following are various considerations to be pondered for initiating and sustaining the practice of the JR Kata. A fundamental understanding of TWI-JR can be attained through the training. Our aim is not to supplant the training in any way. We will, however, concentrate on how to coach and practice the JR Kata after the practitioner has taken the course. We will also describe synergisms between the Toyota Kata and TWI-JR.

6.3 Need for Coaching

As advised in previous chapters, anyone being introduced to a new kata has ostensibly had some level of previous experience practicing the Improvement Kata. Having attained the benefits of repeated practice learned through the Improvement Kata application, the JR Kata novice will be fully prepared for the consistency and rigor that will be demanded.

If the frequency of the JR Kata practice is a determinant of its ultimate utility, then the number of people that any given manager or supervisor oversees is proportional to the opportunity for the kata's application. Supervisors and lower-level managers who directly oversee the work of many value-adders are most likely to have the greatest opportunity to quickly attain expert status.

Depending on management structure and job classification, the JR Kata may quite possibly be the first problem-solving kata a manager learns. Unlike improvement, the investigative process inherent in problem solving can be disconcerting as well as lengthy.[1] Even when a problem surfaces that is seemingly not related to relations, quite often, human-based causes are discovered. The Improvement Kata does not prepare a practitioner for complicated matters of personality. Consequently, skilled coaching of the JR Kata is advised.

6.3.1 Coaching the JR Kata

In Chapter 4, the concept of the internally developed preceptor was introduced. Since the skill of constructively dealing with human relations issues can take years to master, the JR Kata may require coaching by a preceptor. Regardless, those who are chosen to begin JR Kata coaching should be seasoned and skilled in both the Improvement as well as the JR Kata. As a goal, when the vicissitudes of life do trigger contention, all managers should be able to practice the standard interpersonal problem-solving skill that the JR Kata provides.

The TWI-JR trainer manual provides a script used for facilitating the trainee description of the problem. Along with the proper use of the JR four-step method on the card and the application of the JR analysis form, the script completes the adherence to the JR Kata that every manager should flawlessly practice. The process is described as follows.

6.4 Practicing the JR Kata

During the TWI-JR course, participants are invited to describe a past or current relational problem. Figure 6.1 is the standard procedure that the instructor uses for each participant's presentation. This "script" is used in combination with the four-step JR card (Figure 6.2) and the "board work" analysis chart (Figure 6.3). The following explanation will not attempt to re-create the course. The content of the course is best presented in the training. As in the other kata that are a derivative of TWI courses, we will suggest practices that we feel will imprint the problem-solving pattern that the course teaches into the learner.

An essential first step for initiating the JR Kata is addressed in the JR course but is not on the card. This part of the kata requires that the

---

JOB RELATIONS
A SUPERVISOR GETS RESULTS
THROUGH PEOPLE

FOUNDATIONS FOR GOOD RELATIONS

Let Each Worker Know How He/She is Getting Along
　　Figure out what you expect of the person
　　Point out ways to improve

Give Credit When Due
　　Look for extra or unusual performance
　　Tell the person while it's "hot"

Tell People in Advance About Changes that will Affect Them
　　Tell them why if possible
　　Work with them to accept the change

Make Best Use of Each Person's Ability
　　Look for abilities not now being used
　　Never stand in a person's way

PEOPLE MUST BE TREATED
AS INDIVIDUALS

TWI
Institute
www.TWI-Institute.org

HOW TO HANDLE A PROBLEM
DETERMINE OBJECTIVE

STEP 1 - GET THE FACTS
　　Review the record
　　Find out what rules and customs apply
　　Talk with individuals concerned
　　Get opinions and feelings
　　Be sure you have the whole story

STEP 2 - WEIGH AND DECIDE
　　Fit the facts together
　　Consider their bearings on each other
　　What possible actions are there?
　　Check practices and policies
　　Consider objective and effect on individual, group and production
　　Don't jump to conclusions

STEP 3 - TAKE ACTION
　　Are you going to handle this yourself?
　　Do you need help in handling?
　　Should you refer this to your supervisor?
　　Watch the timing of your action
　　Don't pass the buck

STEP 4 - CHECH RESULTS
　　How soon will you follow up?
　　How often will you need to check?
　　Watch for changes in output, attitudes, and relationships
　　Did your action help production?

DID YOU ACCOMPLISH YOUR OBJECTIVE?

Figure 6.1 Job Relations Card, adapted from TWI-Institute.

CONFIDENTIAL JOB RELATIONS Problem Analysis Sheet No. _____

— A Supervisor Gets Results Through People —

Key Points to the Problem				
How the problem came up:	Tipped off	Come to you	Objective	
	Size up	Run into	Target Change	

STEP 1 – GET THE FACTS (Be sure you have the whole story)

Review the record	
Rules and customs	
Individuals concerned	
Opinions and feelings	
Actions taken	

STEP 2 – WEIGH AND DECIDE (Don't jump to conclusions)   Mark ✓ , +, —, 0, etc. Under ACTION, ✓ = Take Action, X = No Action

Fit facts together. Consider bearings on each other.	ACTION	Look for gaps and contradictions in the facts. Consider how the facts relate to each other.	Policies and Practices	Objective	Individual	Group	Production
Possible							
Actions							

STEP 3 – TAKE ACTION (Don't pass the buck)

No.	Self (Responsibility)	Others (Ability)	Supervisor (Authority)	Timing of Action

STEP 4 – CHECK RESULTS (Did your action help production?)

Check Timing:	Day: Time:	Day: Time:	Day: Time:	Day: Time:
Output				
Attitudes				
Relationships				

Did you accomplish your objective?   YES   NO

Reason for not achieving objective: _____
(If the action was poor, consider which item on the card was handled poorly.)

Foundations for Good Relations   Could this problem have been prevented or handled while still small?

Foundations/Items used in this action	
Foundations/Items which could have prevented this problem if used	

— People Must Be Treated as Individuals —

Figure 6.2   Job Relations Problem Analysis Sheet, adapted from TWI-Institute.

Standard Procedure

1. Ask supervisor to tell his problem	Head of table. Does this involve you and somebody who comes under your direction? Have you taken action? Tell us up to final action.
2. How problems come up	In which of the four ways did the problem come up? Where appropriate, stress: you sensed or anticipated a change.
3. Get Objective	Get from supervisor: Something to shoot at. Maybe changed. What do you want to have happen here? Does this problem affect the group? What net results do you want after you have taken action? Get group agreement.
4. Get the Facts	Supervisor first, as he recalls them, offhand. Review subheads with supervisor: use cards.
5. Weigh and Decide	Fit facts—Look for gaps and contradictions with group. Possible action: What facts used(from contributor)? Check practices and policies with supervisor. Check objective first with group, then last with supervisor. Check probable effect on individual, group, production, with supervisor.
6. Balance of Case	Facts used (from supervisor)
7. Check step 3	Subheads—with supervisor Why? How? Timing?
8. Check step 4	Subheads—with supervisor When? How often? What?
9. Check Objective	Supervisor
10. Foundations (if applicable)	Supervisor

(Thank supervisor and clear board except questions and steps.)

Figure 6.3 Standard Procedure in Job Relations Training, adapted from TWI-Institute.

practitioner determine how the problem surfaced. In the course, four possibilities exist:

■ Being tipped off
■ Sizing up before it happens
■ Coming to you
■ Running into

Notice that for the first two possibilities the practitioner is alerted to the concern through active involvement, while for the last two contingencies the concern is received passively. Keeping track of how human relations problems surface is an important indicator of a manager's level of engagement with his or her charges. Some ratio that is designed to reveal a manager's preemptive and reactive relational inclinations can be valuable in analyzing and improving on a manager's people skills.

As with the Improvement and PS Kata, the JR Kata requires the practitioner to identify a target condition. In the JR course, the target condition is identified on the JR card as the objective. Having previously learned the Improvement Kata, the practitioner might be tempted to use the target condition form presented in Chapter 2. As we have learned from the other kata, comparing the target conditions to the actual results (JR card step 4) provides an added feature for reflection. We therefore suggest the use of the target condition form for later comparison to JR Kata results. Be sure to predict changes in output and changes in attitude and relationships, and also ask yourself if your action will help production and if you accomplished your objective. Include these as part of the target conditions (objective) since these questions will be asked at the end of the kata.

6.4.1 Step 1

Step 1 of the JR card, "Get the facts," is similar to the assemblage of current conditions in the Improvement and PS Kata. Again, collecting the pertinent information and going to see in gemba is required. Even though, as described so far, the process in the JR Kata is really no different from the other kata, the TWI-JR training reveals its greatest value as a method for dealing specifically with human feelings and emotion in this step.

The JR course instructs the practitioner to "get opinions and feelings" and to treat them as part of the facts. This is an important point that typical problem-solving kata miss. As said by the instructor in the course, "What a person feels or thinks, right or wrong, is a fact to that person and must be considered as such."[2]

The course provides instructions on how to get opinions and feelings. Again, a comprehensive review is provided in the course, but the main points are as follows:

- Don't argue.
- Encourage the individual to talk about what is important to him or her.
- Don't interrupt.
- Don't jump to conclusions.

- ◼ Don't do all the talking yourself.
- ◼ Listen.

Obtaining this added information and placing it into the Facts column of the analysis chart (Figure 6.3) for consideration during the analysis can prevent a lot of grief later on.

6.4.2 Step 2

Step 2 on the card directs the practitioner to "weigh and decide." Notice that the analysis form includes the wording "possible actions" directly under weigh and decide. The items listed in this column are actually preliminary to deciding. Before weighing significance, the first two entries under step 2 actually refer back to step 1:

- ◼ Fit facts together.
- ◼ Consider their bearings on each other.

A JR Kata coach should make sure that the learner doesn't quickly dismiss these two directives. As JR instructors, we often have to slow down and ask the participants, "By fitting the facts together and considering their bearing on each other, do we understand which of the facts are related, and how? Are the facts associated by sequence? Does the elimination of one fact eliminate another?" In the course, the participants must be challenged on these two points or they will be quickly written off. Often, this line of questioning prompts additional facts from the participants. This same measure should be taken when coaching this kata.

6.4.3 Step 3

Precautions for coaching step 3 include the last two statements in this step. Watch the timing of your action can be tricky. Letting employees vent upon learning about changes is used as an example in the course. Other timing considerations can also include the consideration of weekends, vacations, and holidays as well as grievance, celebratory, and compensation changes. Many other timing considerations exist.

The italicized "Don't pass the buck" is not confined to letting someone else do the hard or dirty work, although that is included. The course includes blaming others for changes that the practitioner must implement as another way of passing the buck.

6.4.4 Step 4

Step 4 directs the practitioner to check results. The first entry under this step states, "How soon will you follow up?" A learner new to the JR Kata but well versed in the Improvement Kata will be tempted to find out, "As soon as possible. Today is not too soon," as step 5 of the Improvement Kata directs (Figure 2.1). As a general rule of thumb, this is probably good advice. Since this type of problem solving is designed for human relations, one must account for the fact that some behaviors are not easily or quickly altered. Consideration of this, based on the circumstances, must be given.

This step then asks the practitioner, "How often will you follow up?" Typically, ongoing confirmation of the situation will be necessary. The directive implies that some determination of frequency for reevaluation is prudent.

6.4.5 Reflection

By having predicted outcomes previous to step 1 above, reflection is facilitated. This is a coaching point that is not made obvious in the JR training but should not be missed! Recall from the Improvement plan–do–check–act (PDCA) cycle sheet in Figure 2.6, the comparison of hypothesis with results is what crystallizes the lesson in the learner's mind. The three entries (changes in output, changes in attitudes, and changes in relationships), the italicized phrase (Did your action help production?), and the footer (Did you accomplish your objective?) on the JR card all provide differing analytical perspectives that should stimulate thorough contemplation.

TWI-JR provides the perfect platform for improving organizational relations. As repeated throughout the book, the training alone is just not enough. Practice is essential for the continued application of the kata. The Toyota Kata contributes to a fuller understanding of the JR Kata by requiring the practitioner to hypothesize outcomes *before* beginning the analysis. The synergisms that the Improvement Kata provides TWI-JR are not one way. The following section will provide an explanation on how TWI-JR contributes to the effectiveness of the Coaching Kata.

6.5 Foundations for Good Relations

Since the objective of the JR Kata is to solve problems, it is necessarily a skill for conducting maintenance kaizen. The TWI-JR course does, however, provide direction on how to promulgate good relations. The Foundations for Good Relations (Figure 6.2) presented in the TWI-JR training are indeed of a preventive nature, but they cannot be considered a kata since they are not a skill learned through a sequenced pattern of repetitive practice. Nonetheless, the foundations are easily modeled during coaching sessions and should be used in conjunction with any instruction or coaching.

Knowledge and a concerted effort by kata coaches to require the use of the foundations by learners, when applicable, can broaden the extent of its use. Coaching the foundations into instruction and coaching will steadily permeate into other segments of the business culture.

Step 4 of the Improvement Kata (Figure 2.1), "What is your next step (start of next PDCA cycle)," provides an excellent example of how the foundations can act to improve a kata practice. The practitioner might be convinced of an improvement's efficacy. If the practitioner is a manager, the instinctive response might be to direct their subordinates to make the change. The third foundation, "Tell people in advance about changes that will affect them," and the two entries that follow it suggest that springing a work modification on those that must adapt to it makes for poor relations.

This foundation, combined with the Improvement Kata emphasis on measured experimentation and rapid PDCA cycling, portends a need to gain consensus first. An initial experiment might involve having a volunteer test the new method. Feedback from the volunteer then becomes part of the Improvement Kata requirement for reflection. Cogent concerns are surfaced, adjustments can be made, and the volunteer will surely communicate his or her feelings to co-workers. A next experiment would likely test the adjusted method more widely. This iterative process prepares the workforce for acceptance and provides them with input.

The foundations, even if not a kata, are a valuable cultural fortifier. TWI-JR is a critical component of the Seven Kata and should be strategically prioritized for adoption based on necessity.

6.6 JR Kata and A3 Thinking

The JR analysis chart shown in Figure 6.3 is another good example of A3 thinking. The chart co-locates all of the pertinent information alongside objectives, data (facts), considerations, and the ultimate countermeasure. As will be detailed in Chapters 7 and 8, the compilation of all significant information into a single glance assists the mind's eye in the consideration of many alternatives. In the same way that an A3 can be used to communicate information to small teams, the JR analysis chart can be similarly applied.

6.5 Conclusion

In Chapter 2, we argue that the Improvement Kata lays Lean's cultural foundation. In this chapter, we have shown how critical a role the JR Kata can play in building a cultural framework. The JR Kata consists of the simultaneous application of JR's standard method, four-step method, and the analysis chart. Together, these components of TWI-JR form a repeatable problem-solving kata that focuses on human relations. As such, the JR Kata should be defined as an important element of maintenance kaizen.

TWI-JR also provides what is referred to as *preventive medicine* in the course. This preventive medicine is the Foundations for Good Relations that were discussed in this chapter. The foundations, although not a kata, do provide a valuable feature for the coaching of any kata. This synergistic effect demonstrates how TWI and the Toyota Kata were cut from the same cloth.

We also discussed the enhancement that the practice of the Improvement Kata reveals to a JR Kata learner. By simply predicting outcomes before gathering information, the learner is able to assess any lessons learned by comparing his or her predictions to the actual results of his or her actions.

We also advised the practice of tracking which of the four ways the problem surfaced as a way to determine any particular supervisor's or manager's level of proactive abilities over less-desirable reactive responses.

We hope that readers and aspiring kata practitioners alike will thoughtfully consider their plan for rolling out the JR Kata.

Chapter 7

Job Safety Kata: The Duplex Kata

The Training Within Industry (TWI) Job Safety (JS) Kata is perhaps the most interesting of the Seven Kata. Each of the other kata has its own unique provenance and characteristics. The JS Kata, however, is more than what might be perceived of at first glance. It is the only one of the Seven Kata that can serve dual kaizen purposes. Depending on the need, the JS Kata can be applied for either improving or problem solving.

Consequently, the JS Kata can be used for improvement kaizen and maintenance kaizen. Certainly, the Job Instruction (JI) Kata supports improvement as well as maintenance kaizen efforts. It just so happens that the function of JI Kata as a standardizing tool is identically applied to both types of kaizen. In contrast, the JS Kata can be applied to prevent a safety incident (improvement kaizen) or can be used as an analytic tool to preclude the recurrence of a past safety incident (maintenance kaizen), depending on how it is applied.

To distinguish which of the two JS Kata we are referring to, for the remainder of this chapter we will identify them individually as the JS Improvement Kata, JS Problem-Solving Kata, or simply as the JS Kata when we mean both.

7.1 JS Improvement Kata

JS was developed to serve as a tool of preemption. The JS card (see Figure 7.1) specifically states, "The meaning of safety is to consider measures and take action **before** a safety incident occurs. It is **NOT** to handle

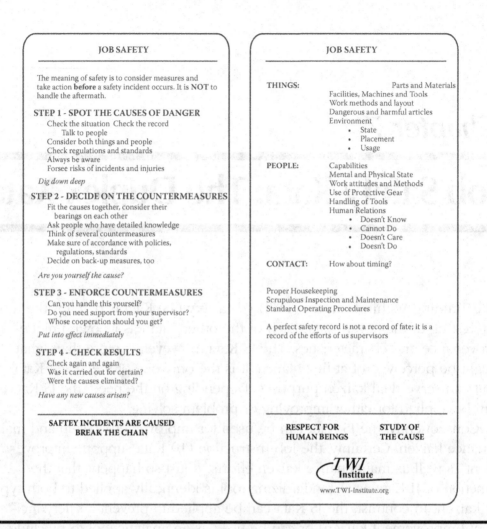

The meaning of safety is to consider measures and take action **before** a safety incident occurs. It is **NOT** to handle the aftermath.

STEP 1 - SPOT THE CAUSES OF DANGER

Check the situation Check the record
     Talk to people
Consider both things and people
Check regulations and standards
Always be aware
Forsee risks of incidents and injuries

Dig down deep

STEP 2 - DECIDE ON THE COUNTERMEASURES

Fit the causes together, consider their
     bearings on each other
Ask people who have detailed knowledge
Think of several countermeasures
Make sure of accordance with policies,
     regulations, standards
Decide on back-up measures, too

Are you yourself the cause?

STEP 3 - ENFORCE COUNTERMEASURES

Can you handle this yourself?
Do you need support from your supervisor?
Whose cooperation should you get?

Put into effect immediately

STEP 4 - CHECK RESULTS

Check again and again
Was it carried out for certain?
Were the causes eliminated?

Have any new causes arisen?

SAFTEY INCIDENTS ARE CAUSED
BREAK THE CHAIN

JOB SAFETY

THINGS: Parts and Materials
           Facilities, Machines and Tools
           Work methods and layout
           Dangerous and harmful articles
           Environment
               • State
               • Placement
               • Usage

PEOPLE: Capabilities
           Mental and Physical State
           Work attitudes and Methods
           Use of Protective Gear
           Handling of Tools
           Human Relations
               • Doesn't Know
               • Cannot Do
               • Doesn't Care
               • Doesn't Do

CONTACT: How about timing?

Proper Housekeeping
Scrupulous Inspection and Maintenance
Standard Operating Procedures

A perfect safety record is not a record of fate; it is a
record of the efforts of us supervisors

RESPECT FOR   STUDY OF
HUMAN BEINGS   THE CAUSE

TWI
Institute
www.TWI-Institute.org

Figure 7.1 Job Safety Card, adapted from TWI-Institute.

the aftermath." We believe this statement is meant to encourage the development of a safety culture based on preventive action. Even though the JS method works wonderfully for the analysis of a past safety incident, managers have an ethical imperative that an ongoing focus on safety incident prevention be maintained.

Most manufacturing organizations have some level of safety consciousness. Invariably, in both the manufacturing and construction environments, the handling and movement of materials is common. If well-thought-out precautions are not taken, this type of regime becomes conducive to human injury and the destruction of property. The TWI-JS training and subsequent use of the JS Improvement Kata by management is an ideal way to minimize the number and severity of safety incidents.

Accordingly, the healthcare environment provides a unique set of safety challenges that can also be addressed using the JS Improvement Kata. Since the JS Kata deals with the injury of personnel and product destruction with equal vigor, the method is readily applicable to the safety of both the healthcare provider and the patient. Again, well-thought-out precautions are key. We believe TWI-JS training and the immediate practice of the JS Kata in a hospital setting is research waiting to happen.

Unfortunately, many nascent and/or small organizations take action only after their first serious safety incident. Required safety training and the deployment of new or additional visual controls are usually the first reaction taken after a major safety incident has occurred. As has been explained previously in this book, training programs reliant on block education have their place. These offerings invariably encourage the *practice of safety*. However, they don't easily translate in the manager's mind into what specific daily activity should be performed and at what frequency (i.e., leader standard work).[1] The JS Improvement Kata is a practice that can be mandated and whose frequency of use can be tracked. For the smaller organization, the development of individuals with JS Improvement Kata capability and the tracking and management of JS Improvement Kata activity is advised.

Customarily, larger and more sophisticated manufacturing organizations and construction general contractors make safety awareness a high priority, and many even perform regularly scheduled safety inspections. These are not bad practices. Even so, these practices alone are not enough. Safety is not something that should be departmentalized. It is an issue that can affect anyone and therefore is a concern that should be addressed by everyone. The "practice" of the JS Improvement Kata is then the way for more people to get actively involved in safety incident prevention. When a kata culture is created, a requirement to use the JS Kata 15 minutes daily, until learned, is a great way to raise employee understanding of safety. It is also an excellent means to accentuate a current safety program without having to retrofit or change any ongoing activities.

We suggest to any organization seriously seeking a way to create a safer work environment the integration of a JS Improvement Kata program into their improvement kaizen (Improvement Kata and Job Methods Kata) activities. The integration of safety into a more comprehensive improvement kaizen program can create synergisms missed if the safety department administers the JS Improvement Kata exclusively.

7.1.1 Step 1

To perform the JS Improvement Kata, the practitioner should have taken the TWI-JS course and be armed with a workplace inspection form (see Figure 7.2) and the JS card (Figure 7.1 above). Step 1 is arguably the most crucial element of the JS Improvement Kata. Step 2, "Decide on countermeasures"; step 3, "Enforce countermeasures"; and step 4, "Check results," are all

WORKPLACE INSPECTION FORM

Workplace: _____   Inspector: _____   Date: _____

	ITEM	WHAT	WHEN	WHERE	WHO	HOW (Unsafe Acts & Conditions)	WHY (Reason)
THINGS	Parts-Materials						
	Facilities-Machines						
	Tools-Fixtures						
	Work Methods						
	Layout						
	Dangerous-Harmful Articles						
	Environment						
PEOPLE	Capabilities						
	Mental-Physical State						
	Work Attitudes						
	Work Methods						
	Use of Protective Equipment (PPE)						
	Handling of Tools						
	Human Relations						
	Other						

ENVIRONMENT: Proper Housekeeping, Scrupulous Inspection and Maintenance, Standard Operating Procedures

Figure 7.2   Job Safety Workplace suggested Inspection Form, adapted from TWI-Institute.

important in performing the kata. If, however, the initial workplace assessment required in step 1 is flawed, the most creative of countermeasures, a stringent adherence to those countermeasures, and the most focused reflection of results can fall short of preventing safety incidents. Thus, close attention to step 1 is made in this section.

On the front side of the card (see Figure 7.1), step 1 directs the practitioner to "spot the causes of danger." Within this step, the card begins with a comprehensive evaluation of the current condition. Step 1 implies that a visit to gemba is warranted and directs the practitioner to "check the situation, check the record, and talk to people." Ostensibly, the practitioner has already developed this skill through practice of the Improvement Kata. Grasping the current condition always begins with observation, reading, and questioning.

Step 1 then guides the practitioner to "consider both things and people." Notice that the reverse side of the card presents four key considerations: things, people, contact, and environment. The first two topics, things and people, correlate to this portion of step 1.

The JS workplace inspection form (Figure 7.2) contains fields for virtually the entire backside of the card. The form emphasizes the "Things" and "People" card entries by applying the Kipling method (see Chapter 8) to each of the factors. Both of us authors have participated in and reviewed workplace safety inspections. Neither of us can recall this type of Socratic interrogative process applied to a workplace safety inspection. We believe this type of analysis is an important element of improvement, one that we discuss at length in the next chapter. The ability to use this form proficiently will be partly due to experience in the performance of the Job Methods (JM) Kata.

Most organizations managing a mature safety program will use some sort of workplace inspection form of their own for safety assessments. The workplace inspection form used in the TWI-JS course is preferred since it is designed to support the use of the JS card. We recommend its use.

During JS training, we have been told by customers that the form is good but their in-house form was designed specifically for their operations. In the spirit of Yokoten (see Chapter 2), the idea behind how the JS card and inspection form coordinate with each other is the concept that should be considered for adoption. The card is used to guide the application of the entire plan–do–check–act (PDCA) cycle. The workplace inspection form is used during the planning phase of the PDCA cycle as a checklist to ensure completeness of the assessment. Any organization already conducting workplace safety inspections should seriously consider integrating TWI-JS tools into their safety system.

7.1.1.1 Things

In consideration of "Things," the TWI-JS instructor manual states that parts and materials "must meet safety standards and conform to proper shape and material selection" as these are characteristics that can cause injury.[2] Sharply shaped corners and edges or easily fractured materials present possible hazards.

The next consideration under "Things" reads: facilities, machines, and tools. Things within the facility like electrical wiring, doors, or plumbing as well as the facility itself should be examined. Machines that are altered or in some way place people or materials at risk should also be assessed. The operation of tools not designed for the way they are used poses risks, as does improper handling or poorly secured equipment.

The next considerations are work methods and layout. The layout or, more parochially, floor plan can contribute to a safe environment. Tight or unintended passageways, equipment placement incompatible to safety, blind corners, and awkward exit and egress are only some layout features that the practitioner should become aware of.

Work methods are another area that should be assessed. For individuals who have practiced the JI Kata, the evaluation of work methods for safety should be easily comprehended. As pointed out in Chapter 3, anything that can injure the worker is considered a job instruction key point and should be documented in the JI breakdown sheet as such. The review of JI breakdown sheets provides the referential support that a JS Improvement Kata practitioner can evoke when observing the work being performed. This is in accordance with Occupational Safety and Health Administration (OSHA) guidelines, which state, "Each site safety and health program will need to include the following:...means or methods for the development and communication to employees of the various plans, work rules, standard operating procedures and practices that pertain to individual employees and supervisors..."[3] The JI Kata works at an elemental level to integrate safer work methods into overall JS Improvement Kata efforts. Having previously learned the JI Kata provides the practitioner an upper hand in learning the JS Improvement Kata.

The next entry in step 1 asks the practitioner to focus on dangerous and harmful articles. This includes the handling and storage of flammable or toxic materials. Close scrutiny should also be placed on any material with explosive, combustible, radioactive, carcinogenic, or even contagious properties.

"Environment" is written on the next line. Further down the card, it is also listed a second time. This first reference to the environment has to do with the previous line's reference to dangerous or harmful articles. Depending on the surroundings, harmful articles can be made more dangerous. The situation may even precipitate behavioral or emotional changes in exposed individuals.

The last three bulleted entries in step 1 are state, placement, and usage. *State* refers to the chemical, physical, or electronic nature of the thing in question. A particular "thing" may be innocuous in one state and highly dangerous in another. Such considerations are common in continuous processes. The *placement* of things is also important for the practitioner to consider. Visual controls reveal abnormal occurrences, such as misplaced things. *Usage* is a broader form of the previously mentioned misuse of machines and tools. Anything can be used incorrectly. As the TWI-JS instructor manual states, "even a stick may become a dangerous weapon depending on its use."

7.1.1.2 People

The "People" section of the JS Improvement Kata demonstrates how indispensable it is to have previous experience in the practice of some of the other kata. Skills are what the Seven Kata are about. Previous application of the JI and Job Relations (JR) Kata will provide the practitioner with the skills necessary for the proper assessment of people-related safety features. This benefit is also taken advantage of by the TWI-PS course.

"Capabilities" is the first entry listed under the heading "People." The TWI-JI training introduces an efficient and effective tool for assessing capabilities. The JI training timetable is a simple matrix that conveys task capability by defining the relationship between an individual to the task proficiency. Chapter 3 provides a treatment of the subject matter. We suggest its use here.

Next, "Mental and physical state" is listed. As TWI trainers, we believe this to mean a sincere interest in people's well-being. The TWI-JR's Foundation for Good Relations (see Figure 6.1) provides guidelines for getting results through people. For us, these guidelines seem to provide the supervisor with the proper set of applicable psychological motivators. Even though effective, they in and of themselves cannot substitute for a genuine concern for each individual's welfare. People's physical state is not only important, but its consideration is a legal requirement that must be considered.

The next entry is, "Work attitudes and methods." Again, the connection to the JI and JR Kata is obvious. In general, *work attitudes* is addressed by

ITEM	INDIRECT CAUSES	DIRECT CAUSES UNSAFE ACTS AND CONDITIONS	INCIDENT	INJURY
			When *who* tried to do *what, how, what happened* and what were the *results?*	(Use numbers if possible) People: Things:
	COUNTERMEASURES			ESTIMATED COST Money: Time: Things: Other:

Figure 7.3   Safety Analysis Table.

the JR Kata, and *methods* involves JI Kata considerations. On the card, the bulleted entries under "People" provide a better indication of how the acquired JI and JR skills will be applied in the JS Kata.

"Use of protective gear" is the next entry. The proper use of personal protective equipment (PPE) would seem to be a no-brainer. Both of us authors work in industrial extension and are frequently in a wide variety of manufacturing environments, so we feel we are in a unique position to provide perspective on this important issue.

Management sophistication usually is the determining factor in the consistent and proper use of PPE. We have worked with many closely held or family businesses in light manufacturing, and in some of these operations the consistent use of PPE was never enforced. What resulted was the near absence of PPE. We've also observed other similar operations within the same industry sector where the required proper use of PPE was nonnegotiable, even for visiting guests. Sometimes, a simple consistent requirement makes all the difference.

The next entry is the "Handling of tools." This concern is primarily a training issue. The TWI-JI training uses an excellent example of how this issue is properly handled. Figure 7.3 is the example used to demonstrate how the Job Instruction breakdown sheet is scalable to skill level. The handling of tools is a key point within the breakdown structure. Also evident is how, even at a higher skill level, the organization's unique method of tool operation can be verified through observation.

The last entry is, "Human relations: Doesn't know, cannot do, doesn't care, doesn't do." To best address each of these contingencies, having received TWI-JI and JR training and extensive practice in their associated kata enables the JS Kata practitioner a learning advantage.

The "Doesn't know" or "Cannot do" bullets call for the instructional skills provided by the JI Kata. The "Doesn't care" and "Doesn't do" bullets can be better understood by applying the JR Kata.

7.1.1.3 Contact

The reason that manufacturing environments are inherently more prone to safety incidents is that by definition, materials at some point are placed into a kinetic regime. Anytime materials and/or equipment are moving, unintended contact can present hazards. The greater the forces involved, the greater the hazard. This section of the card also includes the consideration of the timing of contact and kinetic forces.

Two Sample Job Breakdowns			
Example 1 Job Breakdown for Training		Example 1A Job Breakdown for Training	
Operation: bore, ream and face Part: governor brake disc		Operation: chucking Part: governor brake disc	
IMPORTANT STEPS A logical segment of the operation when something happens to advance the work	KEY POINTS Anything in a step that might— 1. Make or break the job 2. Injure the worker 3. Make the work easier to do, i.e., "knack," "trick," special timing, bit of special information	IMPORTANT STEPS A logical segment of the operation when something happens to advance the work	KEY POINTS Anything in a step that might— 1. Make or break the job 2. Injure the worker 3. Make the work easier to do, i.e., "knack," "trick," special timing, bit of special information
1. Chuck	Chuck squarely—no chips, no nicks	1. Open jaws	Wrench full into sprockets
2. Indicate	Low speed	2. Clean out chips	Use brush—not hands. Get all out
3. Center drill	Angle—give drill double hearing	3. Set piece in jaws	
4. Drill	Lips even. Feed even. High for chip clearance. Clean drill.	4. Adjust jaws to piece	Even pressure all around— not too tight
5. Reverse piece		5. Try for balance	Must center
6. Bore	Feed even and slow	6. Final tighten—jaws	Must hold against pull of cutting tools
7. Plug gauge	Enough stock for reaming	A job setter in a machine shop did this breakdown in 9 minutes. He uses this breakdown "as is" for operators who have had other bench lathe experience. For newcomers, he uses one or two of the above steps as a separate instructing unit and makes a separate detailed breakdown for each of these smaller units.	
8. Ream	Feed evenly. If bell-shaped, check tool		
9. Set cross slide	No backlash		
10. Turn	Feed evenly. Keep "drag" for good finish.		
11. Face	Keep "drag" for finish		

Figure 7.4 Sample Job Breakdowns.

7.1.1.4 Environment

The "Environment" section is all about workplace orderliness, upkeep, and standards. We often remind trainees that a safe factory environment is the same as it is for a restaurant. The trainer will typically recollect a similar operation where, "you could have eaten off the floor!"

Housekeeping is the first indicator that we use to gauge a management team's level of discipline. Housekeeping issues are similar to those discussed concerning the consistent and proper use of PPE. An additional assessment device concerning housekeeping that we use to get a glimpse into the organization's culture is to quickly pop into the restrooms that hourly employees, especially production workers, are required to use. Managers cognizant of and actionable to such minutia usually have the wherewithal to earnestly initiate a Lean journey.

The "Scrupulous inspection and maintenance" entry is the next logical step taken after a robust housekeeping program has been developed. Inspection begins with planned and condition-based maintenance and the use of visual controls. Advancements beyond preventive maintenance include predictive maintenance, reliability maintenance, and value-driven maintenance. Each has their specific characteristics and commonalities.

7.1.2 Observations

As explained with housekeeping and PPE, fiat management can work when properly applied. In short, skills cannot be mandated; they must be taught. Conversely, practices can be mandated and should be.

Before moving on to the application of the JS Problem-Solving Kata, an explanation of the role that JS Improvement Kata plays in preparing the practitioner for the immediate unpracticed use of the JS Problem-Solving Kata is in order.

Over a given period of time, only so many safety incidents will occur. Throughout this book, we have continuously argued that the only effective path to skill proficiency is through repeated practice. Regular practice is impossible with infrequent discrete events, which hopefully is the situation within your organization. Regardless, performing a regularly scheduled "kata" on safety incidents is virtually impossible unless you're a busy OSHA accident investigator.

Providentially, the JS Kata uses the nearly identical process for safety improvement that it does for preventing safety incident recurrence. This means that a practitioner well versed in JS Improvement Kata preventive action should be able to seamlessly transfer that skill into the JS Problem-Solving Kata corrective action if and when the need arises. This is another of many examples of how learning to improve should precede learning the problem-solving process.

7.2 JS Problem-Solving Kata

Review of the Safety Analysis Table (Figure 7.4) reveals that the entire analysis is recorded on what is, for all intents and purposes, an A3. It does not, in and of itself, complete an entire PDCA cycle. It does, nevertheless, possess the unmistakable multipaneled storyboard that is visually concise and contains all of the information gathered within a single eyeshot. In our opinion, the safety analysis table is a good example of A3 thinking.

The safety analysis timetable is ingeniously designed for extracting possible countermeasures from the practitioner's mind. As will be made clear in Chapter 8, the simultaneous consideration of disparate information stimulates innovative (i.e., improvement) thinking. The form facilitates this "out of the box" thought process by co-locating all of the information into a single glance.

If a safety incident has occurred, investigation of the incident becomes key to preventing a recurrence. Accident investigation is a field unto itself, and many training offerings are currently available. The OSHA website even provides a small business reference manual for accident investigation.[4] As with anything else, previous experience with this skill is advantageous.

Accident investigation practices are difficult to simulate, so for educational purposes, case studies are typically resorted to. As an alternative, the JS Kata uses a novel strategy that first develops safety improvement (i.e., incident prevention) skills as the foundation for building problem-solving (i.e., cause elimination) skills. This is exactly the same sequence of learning that we suggest for adopting all Seven Kata; that is, coach improvement before teaching problem solving.

Uniquely, the JS Kata bridges the gap between specialized accident investigation training and the more broad-based safety awareness training. As previously mentioned, safety incident prevention should be everyone's job. TWI-JS training followed by JS Improvement Kata practice offers a practical approach for disseminating safety insight to all. With ardent resolution, any organization whose workforce is faced with a hazardous work environment can achieve its safety goals by shrewdly applying the JS Kata.

In Section 7.1, we focused attention onto step 1 of the front side of the card and the backside of the card in its entirety. The purpose of the backside of the card is to consider everything possible, from many differing perspectives. Consideration of the entire spectrum of possibilities when envisioning potential future safety incidents is vital.

In this section, step 1 remains much the same; however, use of the Safety Analysis Table is included. The workplace inspection form is still used when going to gemba to check the situation, check the record, and talk to people. Step 1 then directs the practitioner to "Consider both things and people (backside of card)." The next item, "Check regulations and standards," can be recorded in either the Other or Environment fields. The form's output is then included into the Items, Indirect, and Direct Causes column and can be of assistance in the use of the Incidents column of the Safety Analysis Table. The Items column becomes fodder for input into the Indirect and Direct Causes columns.

The last two line items in step 1 are "Always be aware" and "Foresee risks of incidents." These two points would not seem to make sense in the context of an accident investigation. They can, nonetheless, still be considered, albeit differently. *Always be aware* is a trait of a kata practitioner that would ostensibly have been learned and practiced in both the Improvement as well as PS Kata. It can be interpreted thusly as a friendly reminder. The JS Problem-Solving Kata practitioner should interpret the "Foresee risks of incidents" line as a pointer of other potential negative effects learned of during the investigation.

We decided to present the remaining three steps of the JS Kata in this section since it is identical for both improvement and problem solving. The stepping stone between step 1 and step 2 is the Safety Analysis Table. After performing step 1, except for the Countermeasures and Estimated Cost fields at the bottom of the form, the entire form should be completed and ready for step 2.

7.2.1 Step 2

Step 2 reads, "Decide on the countermeasure." There are five bullets and an italicized statement under step 2. What follows is a brief discussion of each.

"Fit the causes together. Consider their bearing on each other" is reminiscent of the JR Kata. Recall that in the JR Kata, the analysis is very similar to JS's Safety Analysis Table. In step 2 of the JR Kata, the first line reads, "Fit the facts together. Consider their bearings on each other." These processes are identical, and previous TWI-JR training and practice of the JR Kata places the nascent JS Kata practitioner in the forefront. The completed Safety Analysis Table places all of the items, indirect causes, direct causes, incident, and injury entries into a single amalgamated backdrop. As previously mentioned in this chapter, and which will be reiterated in the next, the co-location of all the available information enhances one's ability to consider seemingly disparate quanta almost simultaneously. This "bottled lightening" is at the heart of all innovation, including improvement.

The next bullet is, "Ask people who have detailed knowledge." Often, workers have the best ideas for countermeasures because they know the work intimately and have most probably thought about the problem at hand. Leads, supervisors, and managers are also valuable assets in the endeavor to develop countermeasures.

Bullet number three reads, "Think of several countermeasures." The main objective of this statement is to keep the practitioner from leaping headlong into a predetermined countermeasure. It is senseless to perform the kata if a previously decided upon countermeasure is going to be used anyway. Although not recommended, it only makes sense to test the preordained countermeasure before using the kata if it has already been chosen. Forcing the consideration of more countermeasures will stimulate an appreciation for overlooked ideas and should therefore be carried out in earnest.

If a countermeasure seems to be viable, bullet number four should be considered. "Make sure of accordance with policies, regulations, standards" is seemingly obvious but can be lost in the rush to fix the problem.

The last bullet under step 2 is, "Decide on next-best measures too." This is closely associated with bullet number three, above. Much like the PS Kata requirement that the practitioner reconsider the root cause three different times before the 5-Why analysis is initiated, this bullet is meant to slow down the practitioner to ponder this decision one more time. The reference to the plural "next-best countermeasures" suggests that a ranking of the countermeasures be determined.

The italicized statement at the end of step 2 reads, "Are you yourself the cause?" This is usually taken to mean that the practitioner might in some way accommodate the tacit acceptance of a causal factor. Outside the context of the JS Problem-Solving Kata, this statement can be taken differently. Since a safety incident has not occurred previous to the use of the JS Improvement Kata, this statement could also be taken as a warning to the practitioner that one's inclinations can bias the result.

7.2.2 Step 3

Step 3 is, "Enforce countermeasures." Obviously, an unused countermeasure is worthless. Occasionally, a countermeasure can be accomplished via a visual control or even an error-proofing device. Some level of retraining may even be needed. More often than not, however, a countermeasure will demand behavior modification. Regardless of what constitutes the countermeasure, acceptance will be required. This is the gist of step 3.

The first bullet in step 3 reads, "Can you handle this yourself?" Personalities differ. Some might be compelled to do it themselves. Others might seek consensus. This bullet requires that the practitioner think about this issue. Perhaps the practitioner can handle it and needn't concern his or her boss. It is also possible that the countermeasure is so broad that others will need to sign off on the change.

Bullet number 2 closely follows the first bullet. "Do you need your supervisor?" If proposed countermeasures require the notification or authorization from other managers at or above the level of the practitioner's supervisor, at the least a briefing is advisable. The countermeasure may also need higher-level backing if it is radically different from what had been previously acceptable. This point is worth contemplative consideration.

The last bullet states, "Whose cooperation should you get?" Much like the JR Kata fifth bullet in step 2, which reads, "Consider objective and effect on individual, group, and production," the practitioner should consider all that will be affected by the countermeasure to determine whose cooperation will be needed.

The italicized statement under Step 3 is reminiscent of the Improvement Kata imperative to cycle through experimental countermeasures as quickly as possible: "Today is not too soon!" The directive, "Put into effect immediately" has a similar air. As previously stated in this book, don't let perfection get in the way of progress. Even though the TWI course doesn't specifically have the trainee cycle through steps 2 through 4 iteratively, previous practice of the Improvement Kata will make apparent the need to cycle through these steps until the desired countermeasure is achieved.

7.2.3 *Step 4*

Step 4 directs the practitioner to "Check results." The fact that the last step of the JS Kata ends on the *check* spot on the PDCA cycle means that the *act and adjust* of PDCA must logically follow. The assumption that steps 2 through 4 are meant to cycle through iteratively is not a stretch. Adjusting obviously means a return to step 2 if the results of the countermeasure are not satisfactory.

Nowhere in the TWI-JS course is the directive given that the practitioner should return to step 2 to improve the countermeasure. We see a clear connection of the JS Kata to the Improvement Kata if step 4 is seen as a precursor to more improvement. This logic is also applicable here to the JS Problem-Solving Kata. We recommend the integration of the Improvement Kata practices of fast and iterative experimental cycles toward the target condition used for the JS Kata.

The first bullet under step 4 states, "Check again and again." This is another indicator of the need for continued iterations back to step 2. This ensures that the practitioner has the opportunity to discover the shortcomings of the countermeasure. If a shortcoming is detected, we suggest a return to step 2 with recently discovered shortcoming "items" available to initiate the process.

The next bullet questions the countermeasure's staying power. "Was it carried out for certain?" and the previous bullet "Check again and again" imply that a return visit to gemba is not only reasonable but also necessary.

The last bullet, "Was the cause eliminated?" is another point for reflection. These three bullets all work synergistically to assess the countermeasure's efficacy. Checking back repeatedly to understand efficacy and acceptance are three features of the reflective mind-set essential to improvement and problem solving.

The italicized statement, "Have any new causes arisen?" indicates a duty to continuously monitor the safety conditions in the area. Situations are constantly in flux, and inadvertent changes will spontaneously occur. These deviations can negate the very countermeasures that were so carefully implemented. Continued monitoring certainly indicates the requirement for ongoing JS Improvement Kata activities.

7.3 JI Kata Connection

JI key points pertaining to safety are an important component of safety. Those portions of a task that are safety sensitive can be readily documented and included in employee training. JI provides for both requirements.[5] The JI breakdown sheet lists all the key points that can injure the worker, and these points are individually addressed during the training of employees that will perform said task.

The combination of built-in safety precautions within the JI breakdown sheet, continuous efforts to identify and eliminate possible incidents through the breakdown sheet revision control process, and the ability to prevent safety incidents from occurring by incorporating newly realized safety concerns into the JI breakdown sheet all provide the foundation for protecting the well-being of the workforce.

7.4 A New 5-Why?

Another interesting detail of the JS Kata is its relationship to an uncommon use of the 5-Why method that we saw applied in the Problem-Solving (PS) Kata in Chapter 5. This novel application of 5-Why analysis is a powerful means of problem solving, one we feel has been overlooked. What follows is what we understand as the connection between this element of the JS Kata and the 5-Why method used in the PS Kata.

The TWI-JS course teaches participants that safety incidents don't just occur in a vacuum, but rather, incidents are caused. In the course, the instructor's board work shows how a causal chain of events is typical of safety incidents. The causal chain described includes indirect causes, direct causes (unsafe acts and conditions), incidents, and injuries (see Figure 7.5). As shown, the JS causal chain analysis is bounded. The JS analysis is indeed related to the more typical open-ended 5-Why investigation in that both are causal chains. What's different is their analytical intent.

Recall from Chapter 5, in step 1 of the PS Kata, that the practitioner is directed to identify the point of cause. The kata then requires consideration of the frequency of the cause. In step 2, the practitioner is again to confirm the point of cause. Up to that point, the PS Kata practitioner has been required to consider the root cause from at least three different perspectives. Only after this repeated deliberation of the root cause is 5-Why analysis introduced. The following point must be made crystal clear! In this different application of 5-Why analysis, the method is not used to identify the root cause, but more accurately, it is used to create a chain of events from the abnormal occurrence (safety incident) to the current condition.

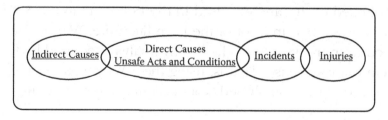

Figure 7.5   The Job Safety Causal Chain, adapted from the TWI-Institute Job Safety manual.

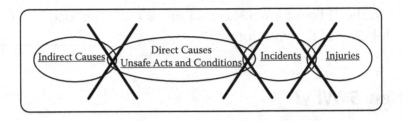

Figure 7.6 The Job Safety Causal Chain, broken, adapted from the TWI-Institute Job Safety manual.

With experience, the reason for re-creating the causal chain of events becomes apparent. Often, the root cause cannot be eliminated. For example, the root cause may be a regulation or even a state or federal law that must be adhered to. In a more traditional organization, managers might throw up their hands and say, "Well, I guess we can't do anything about that!" Truth be told—the possibility of breaking a link in the chain of events, thus preventing the incident, may in fact exist (Figure 7.6). By focusing only on the root cause and neglecting the opportunities to break a critical link in the causal chain of events, many managers miss the potential of eliminating the undesired effect.

As is made clear in the TWI-JS course Safety Analysis Table (see Figure 7.4), safety incidents are typically composed of many chains of events that might occur simultaneously to become manifest. This multichain dynamic is a significant mechanism that is also too often neglected in the typical 5-Why analysis. The entire identification and eventual bounding of the chain of events is only one of perhaps many chains of events associated with the problem. If, per chance, action on the first chain identified does not prevent the problem from recurring, the practitioner can choose another possible root cause and repeat the process in steps 1 and 2.

Interestingly, the TWI-JS course was developed by Toyota, and the PS Kata and Toyota's Practical Problem Solving are very nearly identical.[6,7] It is no coincidence that the 5-Why method used by the PS Kata is more like the "bounded chain" analysis used in the JS Kata than the 5-Why root cause analysis described in most of the Lean literature. Without perspectives gleaned from the JS course, the 5-Why analysis required by the PS Kata doesn't seem to make sense. That is, using the 5-Why analysis after the root cause has already been established would seem to be redundant.

7.5 Conclusions

The duplex JS Kata can be applied uniquely to perform either improvement or problem-solving activities. It bridges the gap between general safety awareness training and highly specialized accident investigation training. It works synergistically with the JI nested Kata to produce a comprehensive safety program. The JS Kata card contains the telltale signs of the iterative PDCA cycle that is imprinted upon learning the Improvement Kata. These and many other reasons make the JS Kata an intricate, but infinitely interesting, kata to master.

Chapter 8

Job Methods Kata: Kipling's Kata

I have six honest serving-men
(They taught me all I knew);
Their names are What and Why and When
And How and Where and Who.[1]
—Rudyard Kipling

8.1 Introduction

The Training Within Industry (TWI) Job Methods (JM) training teaches, in the most effective way possible, the understanding of how the Kipling method, also known as the 5W1H, ECRS (what, why, where, when, who, how or how much; eliminate, combine, rearrange, simplify), works (Figure 8.1). The goal of the JM course is to provide the trainee a working knowledge of this analytical approach. This method is still a part of the Toyota Business Practice (TBP) training curriculum and has important specialized applications.[2] As we have repeatedly declared throughout this book, the utility of any acquired skill, including JM, will only manifest if practiced. We therefore include the TWI Job Methods skill as the Seventh Kata in our desire to see its potential fully realized.

Continued practice of the JM Kata by the learner is an essential requirement that is often overlooked by management. As an example, design engineering protocol may lend itself to JM's frequent use as part of, say, a customer-required program review process. More typically though, work of a less technical nature demands a higher level of management involvement to ensure the JM Kata proper application. The learners will only be able to proficiently execute the skill consistently if they are given the opportunity to learn it through regular practice. This requires management prioritization, planning, monitoring, and follow-through.

A somewhat ethereal component to the JM Kata exists that is not evident in the other six kata. In the previous chapters, impact from the katas is shown to be a linear cause-and-effect relationship. The practitioner provides input by performing the defined kata, and as a result, it produces an expected output. The JM Kata often obtains similar results but can also produce surprising step-function improvements to processes. None of the other six kata are designed for that purpose.

The "magic" of the JM Kata has its roots in philosophical inquiry. The philosophers of ancient times used logic as a means of scientific investigation. One early discovery was a questioning approach that we know of today as the Socratic method.[3] The Socratic method takes on many forms, but the basic premise lies in the application of an interrogative process upon a subject. Just as demonstrated in Chapter 5, where the PS Kata was shown to require the full consideration of different perspectives to elicit unthought-of solutions, JM's 5W1H, ECRS analysis provides for a ratcheting of discernment by applying an interrogative cycle of questioning to every single detail of a process. The potential step-function improvement of the JM Kata lies in the recombination and elimination of multiple elements of the work, multiplying the output's impact.

8.2 Relationship of the Improvement and JM Kata

First of all, both the Improvement Kata and TWI-JM are important components of improvement kaizen. As described in Chapter 2, effective use of the Improvement Kata requires value stream analysis (VSA) as a way of focusing improvement activities. The VSA actually serves dual purposes. It not only provides prioritization of improvement activity by the identification of process and pacemaker loops, but it also provides direction for the choice of Improvement Kata target conditions.

The TWI-JM analysis can be similarly applied to any stable process. As such, the consequential redistribution of work elements may require more elemental improvement activity. The Improvement Kata is a practical way of accomplishing this objective. Daily Improvement Kata activity can derive from JM proposal submissions. In coordination, individual Improvement Kata target conditions can address the changes proposed from the JM analysis.

Step 3 of the Improvement Kata states, "What obstacles are now keeping you from the target condition? Which are you addressing now?" Steps 1 (Define the current condition) and 2 (Define the target condition) should have already been conducted using the JM analysis. The individual kata can then pick up with the obstacle that will be addressed.

8.3 Coaching

As Figure 8.1 shows, each detail is subjected to 5W1H, ECRS interrogation. The JM Kata is the painstaking, question-by-question examination of every single detail within the process. This kata in particular has an almost rhythmic mantra. The repetition can quickly become mechanical and lull the learner into a dismissive mindset. This process often unintentionally circumvented is due to a lack of learner discipline. Mastering the JM Kata requires an attentive state of mind. Coaching of the JM Kata is required to instill this skill into the learner's mind.

A common learner mistake is trying to fit a preconceived improvement idea into the JM analysis. Another mistake is listing details without performing or at least witnessing the work. Mistakes are also made by not fully concentrating due diligence during the proposal preparation. A well-written proposal can positively influence improvement kaizen activity. Selection of the process to be analyzed is a crucial issue that goes back to the VSA.

8.4 Proposals and the Nascent Teian Program

The TWI-JM training provides instruction on the writing and submission of improvement proposals. As a matter of workforce-level improvement kaizen, kaizen teian is an important Lean tool that should be managed. Kaizen teian was briefly mentioned in Chapters 2 and 5. As it pertains to Lean improvement kaizen, we believe the adroit management of a robust proposal system is a premier indicator of organizational "Leanness." As a proposal system, kaizen teian is probably one of the most sensitive indicators of a healthy Lean system. The teian system is hypersensitive to management or organizational dysfunction and will degenerate quickly from inattentiveness. Managers' absence from gemba and the loss of the associated interaction that is common to the kata can make the workforce reluctant to tender proposals.

JM teaches learners how to prepare proposals, which are an important but all too often neglected Lean workforce skill. Managers that have written their own JM proposals with the obligation to defend them to an improvement committee come to understand the important features of written proposals. With any experience in coaching the other kata, it is reasonable to expect that these managers could become skillful at coaching proposal writing to their charges.

8.5 JM Kata

This section is not an attempt to provide the reader with the skill developed by taking the TWI-JM training and the subsequent practice of its Kata. By having taken the course, however, it is our hope that we can provide the reader with a fresh insight that will tie together Lean concepts, the TWI-JM training, and the JM Kata. The first part of this section will focus on the actual analysis, and the second part will stress the importance of the implementation strategy. We will conclude by reasserting the JM Kata prescription to continually improve.

8.5.1 JM Analysis

The top of the JM card states its intention: "Job Methods is a practical plan to help you produce greater quantities of quality products in less time, by making the best use of manpower, machines, and equipment now available." Regardless of its anachronistic gender deafness, the card is clear—JM is about productivity improvement. This statement should be included as part of the JM Kata by reciting it daily when beginning its practice.

If the statement is taken literally, it would seem that JM does not apply to transactional processes or services. We should, however, understand "products" to include the delivery of services. Through the many years that both of us have taught the JM course, we have seen it usefully applied to transactional as well as service-oriented processes with great success.

Step 1 instructs the practitioner, "Break down the job." Step 1 also includes the following:

List all details of the job exactly as done in the present method.
Be sure every detail includes all:
  – Material Handling
  – Machine Work
  – Hand Work

Ostensibly, the practitioner has good aptitude with the Improvement Kata, so *going to see* should be nothing new. In fact, previous experience with the Improvement Kata should make the learner new to JM an excellent observer. Much like the current condition analysis performed in the Improvement Kata, the JM Kata requires close attention be paid to the *details* of the job. In contrast, the Improvement Kata requires the additional collection of quantitative data.

Steps 2 and 3 work synergistically to provide an insightful assessment of the process. Step 2 of the JM Kata directs the practitioner, "Question every detail." It goes on to describe the specific questions to be asked and in what order. The questioning sequence is applied to every detail. The questions are as follows:

■ Why is it necessary?
■ What is the purpose?
■ Where should it be done?
■ When should it be done?
■ Who is best qualified to do it?
■ How is the "best way" to do it?

As each of these questions is asked of every detail, the practitioner is directed to simultaneously question: materials, machines, equipment, tools, product design, workplace layout, movement, safety, and housekeeping. This means that 60 different considerations should be given to each and every detail. Understandably, opportunities are easily missed if the practitioner grows weary of the repetitive questioning and begins passing over details, questions, or special considerations.

Step 3 relates each question in step 2 into an associated supposition. Figure 8.1 depicts the relationship between step 2 (5W1H) and step 3 (ECRS). A clarification of the meaning of ECRS is as follows:

- Eliminate unnecessary details.
- Combine details when practical.
- Rearrange details for better sequence.
- Simplify all necessary details.

Figure 8.2 illustrates what the mechanics of the process looks like. It cannot, however, reveal how idea generation development occurs. The JM Kata, specifically steps 2 and 3, provides the practitioner a way to arouse idea concepts that may be arbitrarily dismissed without this analysis. The JM Kata provides a comprehensive, detailed, and orderly method for contemplating the many different contributions and shortcomings of every process component.

While the nexus between steps 2 and 3 stimulates the creative process, the third step provides the dispositive action for each process detail. All the practitioner need do is input the detail into the questioning algorithm and follow it. Answering each question requires rapid thinking. If, for example, one is required to process 37 details through the mental algorithm within 15 minutes, answers to each question for every detail—not to mention the additional consideration of special conditions (materials, machines, equipment, etc.)—will require a lot of mental activity. Innovation (improvement) is

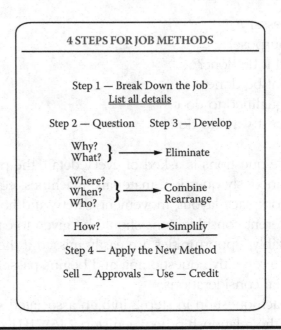

Figure 8.1

HOW TO IMPROVE JOB METHODS

A practical plan to help you produce *greater quantities of quality products in less time* by making the best use of the **Manpower, Machines and Materials now available.**

STEP 1 - BREAK DOWN THE JOB

1. List all details of the job **exactly** as done in the **Current Method**.
2. Be sure details include everything
   - Material Handling
   - Machine Work
   - Hand Work

STEP 2 - QUESTION EVERY DETAIL

1. Use these types of questions:
   WHY is it necessary?
   WHAT is its purpose?
   WHERE should it be done?
   WHO is best qualified to do it?
   HOW is the 'best way' to do it?
2. Question the following at the same time:
   Materials, Machines, Equipment Tools,
   Product Design, Workplace Layout,
   Movement, Safety, Housekeeping

TWI Institute
www.TWI-Institute.org

STEP 3 - DEVELOP THE NEW METHOD

1. **ELIMINATE** unnecessary details
2. **COMBINE** details when practical
3. **REARRANGE** details for better sequence
4. **SIMPLIFY** all necessary details
   To make the job easier and safer to do:
   - Put materials, tools and equipment into the **best position** and **within convenient reach** for the operator
   - Use **gravity feed hoppers** or **drop delivery chutes** whenever possible
   - Make effective use of **both hands**
   - Use **jigs or fixtures** instead of hands
5. Work out your ideas WITH OTHERS
6. WRITE UP the proposed new method

STEP 4 - APPLY THE NEW METHOD

1. SELL your proposal to the boss
2. SELL the new method to the operators
3. Get FINAL APPROVAL of all concerned on Safety, Quality, Quantity, Cost, etc.
4. PUT the new method TO WORK. Use it until a **better** way is developed.
5. Give CREDIT where credit is due

Figure 8.2   Job Methods Card, adapted from TWI-Institute.

driven by the simultaneous consideration of many unrelated concepts. The rapid-fire questioning of the JM Kata most closely simulates innovation by placing different concepts into close proximity.

The fourth part of step 3, "Simplify," provides a convenient array of ergonomic tips that are noted in Figure 8.2. It makes sense that overburden (*muri*) and unevenness (*mura*) are minimized or eliminated when considering simplification.

Common TWI-JM trainee mistakes are mentioned in Section 8.3 of this chapter. As mentioned, a common error that deals with both steps 2 and 3 specifically is cycling through these two interconnected steps thoughtlessly. This and the common mistakes previously mentioned can, nonetheless, be worked through with proper coaching and the practice that the kata provides. Reviewing Figure 8.3 and its complexity can give some insight as why these mistakes can happen if the proper coaching mentioned doesn't occur.

Job Breakdown Sheet

Product: Microwave Shields
Operations: Inspecting, Assembly, Riveting, Stamping and Packing
Made By: Ann Adams
Dept: Riveting and Packing
DATE: xx-xx-xx

Detail No.	Current/Proposed Method Details	Distance traveled in feet	Remarks — Time/Tolerance/Rejects/Safety	Why-What	Where	When	Who	How	Ideas — Write Them Down, Don't Try To Remember.	Eliminate (Unnecessary details)	Combine (details when)	Rearrange - details (for better sequence)	Simplify (All necessary details)	Detail No.
1	Walk to supply box containing copper sheets	6 ft	Already been carried by the material handler	x					No, if sheets nearer bench	x				1
2	Pick up 15 to 20 copper sheets							x	Close to riveter. Better way			x	x	2
3	Walk to the bench	6ft		x					Same as # 1					3
4A	Inspect 12 copper sheets		Rejects with dents & scratches go into scrap bin			x		x	Inspect just before assembly. Better way			x	x	4A
4B	Lay out 12 copper sheets			x					Lay out. Same as #1	x			x	4B
5	Walk to supply box and replace extra sheets	6ft		x					Same as # 1	x			x	5
6	Walk to supply box containing brass sheets	3ft		x					Same as # 1	x				6
7	Pick up 15 to 20 brass sheets					x			Same as # 2			x	x	7
8	Walk to bench	6ft		x					Same as # 1	x				8
9A	Inspect and lay out 12 brass sheets		Rejects with dents & scratches go into scrap bin			x		x	(9A) Inspect: Same as # 4A			x	x	9A
9B	Lay out 12 brass sheets		Place them on top of copper sheets	x					(9B) Lay out: Same as # 4B	x			x	9B
10	Walk to supply box and replace extra sheets	6ft		x					Same as # 1	x				10
11	Walk to bench	6 ft		x					Same as # 1	x				11
12	Stack 12 sets near the riveter			x					No, if lay out not required	x				12
13	Pick up a set of sheets with the right hand							x	Better way				x	13
14	Line sheets together and position them in riveter		Line up tolerance is 5/1000 in.					x	Better way				x	14
15	Rivet the top left corner							x	Better way				x	15
16	Slide sheets to left and rivet top right corner							x	Better way				x	16
17	Turn sheets and position them in the riveter							x	Better way				x	17
18	Rivet the bottom right corner							x	Better way				x	18
19	Slide sheets to left and rivet bottom left corner							x	Better way				x	19
20	Turn sheets around as you lay them on the bench							x	Better way				x	20
21	Stamp "TOP" and stack them on work bench		Stamp on the bottom right corner	x					Find out	x				21
	Repeat items 13 to 21, 11 times													
22	Put 12 sets of shields into the carrying box				x		x		Anytime, anywhere, anyone after riveting		x			22
23	Carry full box to the scale and weigh it	50ft	From bench to scale	x					Not necessary to weigh	x			x	23
24	Fill out a measuring slip and place it in box		Total weigh 40 lbs	x					Not necessary to weigh	x			x	24
25	Take the carrying box to the packing area	100ft	Carried by the material handler		x		x		Anytime, anywhere, anyone after riveting			x	x	25
26	Unload the shields from the box		Unloaded by the packer		x		x		Anytime, anywhere, anyone after riveting		x		x	26
27	Put 200 sets of shields into the packing box		Inspection; packing box handled by packer		x		x		Anytime, anywhere, anyone after riveting		x		x	27
28	Enclose box and write out address slip on it				x		x		Anytime, anywhere, anyone after riveting				x	28
29	Fill out a delivery slip				x		x		Anytime, anywhere, anyone after riveting				x	29
30	Store it until it is delivered		Empty boxes are delivered by the material handler		x		x		Anytime, anywhere, anyone after riveting				x	30

Figure 8.3 Job Methods Breakdown Sheet sample, adapted from TWI-Institute.

8.5.2 Nemawashi and A3 Thinking

The Japanese word *nemawashi* means preparing the ground for planting. In the context of the JM Kata, part of step 3 and all of step 4 focus on "preparing the groundwork for implanting change." The remainder of the JM Kata is what is often referred to in Lean parlance as the nemawashi process.

Part five of step 3 recommends that the practitioner "work out your ideas with others." Unlike step 4, which implores the practitioner to "sell" the idea, working out ideas implies the give and take of an open discussion best taken up with the individuals that know and do the work. Notice that working out the ideas is in step 3—"Develop" the new method. What the card is clarifying is that the analysis alone is not good enough during the development stage. Other interested parties should also be consulted during development!

The last part of step 3 is, "Write up the proposed new method." Figure 8.4 depicts the proposal format presented in the TWI-JM course. In that course, we tell participants that many good ideas have gone untried because they were never written down. Not only does a written proposal supply authorizing managers with a takeaway for later review, but as the proposal is written, it also provides the author an opportunity to focus on the case for change. Written proposals also afford the organization the opportunity to archive ideas for later reference.

A3s are visual management tools that have gained in popularity within the Lean community for applications as diverse as problem solving, improvement kaizen, and project management as well as the catch-ball and nemawashi processes used in hoshin kanri. There is no single correct format for an A3. They all do, however, conform to plan–do–check–act (PDCA) thinking and are customized to visually communicate an incidence.

Conrad is somewhat of a TWI fundamentalist and loathes changing most anything in the Job Methods course from what we initially learned from Patrick Graupp and the TWI Institute. We don't advocate introducing the A3 format into the proposal process taught in the course as some sort of curriculum upgrade. Even so, we do recognize the similarity of the JM proposal form and an A3 document. If A3 thinking is a communication standard widely practiced within an organization, JM trainees from that organization will be easily able to translate the JM proposal form into an appropriate A3 configuration.

Upon further examination of the JM proposal sheet, one can identify all of the fundamental elements of an A3. Ownership, summary, current conditions, and target conditions are all evident in both. A3 provides the added

Improvement Proposal Sheet

Submitted to:
Made by: Department:
Product/Part   Date:
Operations:

The following are proposed improvements on the above operations.

1. Summary

2. Results

	Before Improvement	After Improvement
Production (one worker per day)		
Machine Use (one machine per day)		
Reject Rate		
Number of Operators		
Other		

3. Content

NOTE: Explain exactly how this improvement was made. If necessary, attach present and proposed breakdown sheets, diagrams, and any other related items.

Figure 8.4   Proposal format from TWI-JM course.

benefit of a visually engaging representation of the PDCA cycle. A3s are often described as paneled storyboards since they convey the sequence of events that occurs in and around the PDCA cycle—for all intents and purposes, a story. The pervasive use of charts and graphs in place of prose in A3s adds another dimension of visuality to the A3 storyboard that enhances communication and levels understanding.

Step 4, "Apply the new method," provides the template for implementing the improvement. In step 3, the practitioner is directed to prepare a proposal. The proposal preparation process is what readies the practitioner to do the following:

■ Sell your proposal to the boss.
■ Sell the new method to the operators.
■ Get final approval of all concerned on safety, quality, cost, and so forth.
■ Put the new method to work. Use it until a better way is developed.
■ Give credit where credit is due.

Selling the idea, getting approvals, and making it work with the people involved all takes special preparation, a level of groundwork that is facilitated by the preparation of a proposal.

The need to prepare for selling the new method to bosses and operators alike is obvious. After having gone through this process, the practitioner will have made considerations within the proposal for all concerned (safety, quality, cost, etc.). The proposal preparation also provides the practitioner a chance to recognize those that have assisted in some way.

8.5.3 Continuous Improvement

Some attention should be paid to the statement on the card that asserts, "Use it until a better way is developed." These eight words represent what is probably the most neglected concept in all of the JM Kata. Continual improvements are expected. If per chance, another application of the JM Kata does not immediately follow, the practitioner should resume practice of the Improvement Kata until another opportunity for use of the JM Kata surfaces.

Also, like with kaizen events, just because the analysis has been performed and should work, there's no guarantee that it will. The practitioner should follow up with the Improvement Kata on the JM proposal. The Improvement Kata can be either the long-term vision for the customer or the nearer-term challenge or target condition of an Improvement Kata cycle.

8.6 Conclusion

The JM Kata is an important enhancement to the TWI-JM course. Without its managed application, especially when first introduced into the organization, its usefulness will diminish. The JM Kata provides an important contribution to improvement kaizen activities.

As twenty-first century denizens, it is easy for us to disregard the wisdom of past generations in favor of most things modern. The ancient Greeks used their version of the interrogative method that the JM Kata applies so they could understand the world around them. Kipling reconciled the whole concept of the JM method with his pithy rhyme. We would be foolhardy to discount this important epoch of humanity's scientific heritage.

Chapter 9

Submit to the Kata

Experience in industrial extension has provided perspective. We are no longer amazed when management short-changes activities that will provide outcomes it claims it desires. We believe that this is due to inconsistency. A lack of daily continuity is the true mean destroyer.

Stephen Covey's "7 Habits" comes to mind when explaining inconsistent practice.[1] Covey details the four-quadrant activity-management paradigm shown in Figure 9.1. More often than not, Lean initiatives falter because they are placed into quadrant two, important but not urgent. This book has described kata from many perspectives. The descriptors Covey offers in quadrant two almost perfectly define a kata. At its most simple, kata requires daily activity toward the goal of becoming Lean.

We also believe that too many initiatives tackled simultaneously will detract from them all. We've worked with organizations that had the best of intentions and were sold on Lean's concepts, agreeing that a Lean initiative was the correct path. Upon initiating Lean efforts, we found information technology (IT) solutions were also included as part of their improvement mix. This always reminds us of a pertinent quote by Bill Gates, "The first rule of any technology used in a business is that automation applied to an efficient operation will magnify the efficiency. The second is that automation applied to an inefficient operation will magnify the inefficiency."[2] Work flows should be optimized or at least stabilized before IT solutions are brought to bear.

Far too many struggle with IT initiatives that have little chance for success. The organization must first recognize and understand their throughput deficiencies before seeking technology solutions. Operations must provide

	Urgent	**Not Urgent**
Important	**Urgent & Important** This is where we spend most time "Firefighting" **1**	**Not Urgent but Important** This is where we SHOULD spend most time "Quality time" **2**
Not Important	**3** **Urgent but Not Important** This is what we should be managing "Distraction"	**4** **Not Urgent & Not Important** This is what we should be delegating or getting rid of "Time Wasting"

Figure 9.1 Stephen Covey's Four Quadrants.

a level of predictability that software is able to track. Only then can an IT solution produce the astounding results that software companies promise. Managers that don't understand how to improve throughput will typically seek an IT quick fix that plainly doesn't exist.

The proper acquisition of skills and the informed application of tools and techniques is the answer. The parable of the tortoise and the hare is germane. Unless an organization is offering an item or service that cannot be easily replicated, organizational leadership must accept that the tortoise has the best strategy. It is this strategy that demands submission to the kata.

It is our sincere hope that leaders will quickly come to appreciate this maxim while yielding daily to the way of the Seven Kata.

9.1 First Things First

The comprehensive application of all Seven Kata by any organization can be a daunting task. Initiating efforts with only three of the kata is manageable. As mentioned in previous chapters, the Improvement Kata, the Job Instruction (JI) nested Kata, and the Coaching Kata are the logical starting point for most organizations.

As described, the Seven Kata provide the skill set needed for a Lean transformation. Chapter 1 focused on what an economic warrior is and how the assembly of skills is the recipe for organizational, or for that matter, economic, success. We now understand that Taiichi Ohno was himself an economic warrior and was the driving principal of the Toyota Production System.

In Chapter 2, the Improvement Kata was shown to be the starting point for any Lean journey. An organization must prioritize improvement as the workforce's main point of convergence. This has been known since Lean's first quickening. Anyone with a basic understanding of Lean accepts that kaizen means continuous improvement. Up until Mike Rother's recent Improvement Kata revelation, actually performing kaizen has been inscrutable.

We know of no organization currently on a Lean journey that has started with kaizen as their main objective. They may have identified a constraint and applied a kaizen event to it, but such events are abbreviated and not conducive to continuous improvement.

Top managers may identify with the principles of gemba kaizen and commence gemba walks or applying *genchi gembutsu* (go and see) but again, such actions are only a part of the whole. An organization may try to engage the workforce in idea generation using kaizen teian. As sensitive an indicator as teian is to assessing an organization's Leanness, in and of itself it does not make an organization Lean.

Kaizen has been the vexing challenge that most all of the pursuers of Lean have failed to capture. Only now, with a full appreciation of the Improvement Kata, is improvement kaizen given substance, form, and formula. The Lean community has been using an incomplete and deceptive map to guide their Lean efforts. Comparatively, the Improvement Kata provides a kind of GPS system that can furnish specific directions, charting a path for an organization's Lean journey.

Chapter 3 described the only true way to build instructional and coaching ability within an organization. The improvement skill that the Improvement Kata provides and excellent instructional abilities developed by JI nested

Kata practice are a winning combination that stand as the most necessary skills needed for Lean transformation.

Spear and Bowen identified four rules in their article "Decoding the DNA of the Toyota Production System." Rule number four states, "Any improvement must be made in accordance with the scientific method, under the guidance of a teacher, at the lowest possible level in the organization."[3] The Improvement Kata provides the scientific method through its application of plan–do–check–act (PDCA) cycling. The JI nested Kata develops teachers within the organization necessary for disseminating the improvement.

One-on-one on-the-job training (OJT) is the most effective method of skill development within any organization. The JI nested Kata provides this capability to anyone willing to practice it. Too many organizations rely on the sheer wit of their instructors for the transmission of skill. Most organizations don't even understand the costs of poor instruction and are unaware of the need to codify their instructional efforts.

Improvement and instructional skills are at the heart of Lean, and any efforts at using Lean tools without these skills are a hit-or-miss proposition. Most responsible business decision makers would never take incalculable chances on most aspects of their business, but this is exactly what they do when attempting a Lean transformation. Without providing the workforce the skills necessary to operate a Lean management system, such efforts are fruitless.

All the other kata are hence subordinate to these first two most important kata.

The Coaching Kata will not be mastered by anyone unfamiliar with the quintessential instructional skill learned practicing the JI nested Kata. Chapter 4 provided insight into how coaches are developed. The chapter also mentioned the development of preceptors.

Improvement and JI Kata coaches with a working knowledge of Lean's tools and techniques can become excellent preceptors for the organization. To be sure, an organization can begin their Lean journey without preceptors and still become Lean through the diligent practice of the Improvement and JI nested Kata. Preceptors do, however, provide a leg up for the organization because they can guide learners toward known Lean solutions.

Properly finishing any problem-solving effort without the creative process of countermeasure development learned from the Improvement Kata can become a burden. Solutions to human relations problems can also be difficult without an appreciation of the Improvement Kata process.

The Job Methods (JM) Kata gains immeasurable context with a fully developed understanding and appreciation for the Improvement Kata.

Finally, the Job Safety (JS) Kata dual character can only be appreciated by having first practiced improvement.

As has been made abundantly clear, to fully grasp all of Lean's nuances, a specific skill set is required. This skill set becomes obvious only by understanding and practicing the Seven Kata, and the framework for this practice begins with the Improvement and JI nested Kata.

9.2 Adaptive Learning

For all the process improvement techniques available, used as strategic tools, they fail more often than not. Even when a management team demands better performance and deploys the latest tools and techniques, organizations can expect only marginal results from such mandates. The smaller daily problems that inevitably surface will drive the workforce to create "workarounds." A workforce that lacks standard problem-solving skills will unintentionally damage the carefully engineered system that management hoped would last. So what can be done? How can an organization escape the fate of eventual system dysfunction?

The answer to this quandary lies in the organization's ability to build an adaptable workforce. Adaptive learning is the holy grail of improvement, and the Seven Kata are adaptability's secret sauce.

For any improvement effort to remain sustainable, ongoing improvement is of paramount importance. We have many times discussed continuous improvement and agree, "If it's not improving, it will only get worse—maintenance does not exist." Typically, management doesn't recognize much less have the detailed knowledge necessary to do anything about this system "backslide." Since management rarely performs the value-added activity, it is management's responsibility to make positive change, not the workforce's. If properly prepared, management can perform its role as the engine for continual improvements.

Two things must happen for a continual improvements regime to thrive. The organization must first be able to continually adapt elements within the system based on changing circumstances in order to improve it. Unfortunately, this is where most organizations cease their adaptability efforts. The second requirement is to build a workforce that is itself adaptable. Even more unfortunate, most organizations are completely ignorant of this fact. Regardless of the ingenuity of any improvement, if the individuals performing the work do not adapt, the improvement will not succeed. At Toyota, different versions of the Seven

Kata have been successfully used for at least 50 years, yet the brain science behind kata success is only now beginning to reveal why it works so well.

Within the last 15 or so years, myelin theory has increased our understanding of skill development. We all know that the brain is a complex electrochemical system that has the amazing capability of learning. For a more parochial understanding, brain *gray matter* has been assumed to be at the center of learning and thinking. Actually, the network of neural pathways is what connects the dots in terms of cognitive ability. This neural network is also electromagnetic and therefore requires some sort of insulating material for superior proficiency. This insulating material is myelin, or *white brain matter.*

If the coordination of brain signals is what produces skill, then the insulating effects of myelin is what regulates the signal strength and the timing of those electrical impulses.[4] The brain's ability to control signal strength and precisely synchronize those signals is what helps build skill. So, skills are essentially cognitive. A previous conditioning of brain signals, which in turn directs the neuromuscular system to behave accordingly, even shapes athletic skill through the concept of muscle memory. The term, muscle memory however, is figurative, and naturally, the brain is what is doing the remembering.

With every successive practice session, myelin wraps itself around the appropriate neuron or neurons to secure that pathway for later use. The thicker the myelin wrap, the more enhanced the skill becomes. As engineers, we seek to apply repeatable phenomena to processes and systems, even if science can't completely explain it. Myelin theory does go a long way in giving us some level of understanding on how skills are developed through focused frequent repetition.

It seems, then, that failures and faltering are what learning is all about. Every time we fail, we naturally learn how not to fail again; in essence, we learn to perform a skill correctly. Forcing small failures and having the learner continuously correct them is also a source of the wrapping or growth of myelin around the neuron. The kata purposely use failure and struggle as the fastest and most effective way to skill acquisition.

Since skill and mastery are closely associated, one must be patient and spend the time necessary for the skill to become a natural behavior. There is, however, no shortcut; and therefore it must be repetitively practiced. It's also important to realize that a skill can be lost if the skill is not continually practiced.

Adaptive learning is the keystone to how and why kata works. Through our exploration of the *Toyota Kata*, Daniel Coyle's book *The Talent Code*[5] became required reading. *The Talent Code* centered on our current understanding of myelin theory in explaining talent and adaptability. In recent discussions with Mike Rother, author of *Toyota Kata,* we learned that his latest discussions with brain scientists have helped him understand that there's much more to it than just myelin theory.

Mike Rother tells a story of experiments using CT scans that indicate increased brain activity when college students are asked to constantly text message during the scan. From solely a myelin theory perspective, this increased activity is ostensibly the acquisition of myelin wrapping around neurons, thus coordinating brain signals for learned proficiency.

Interestingly, older adults were also scanned performing the same task. Some did indeed exhibit the same high levels of learning activity. Conversely, other older adults performing the same task did not. Those that did not show higher brain activity and did perform the tasks were asked about their experience. A common thread was boredom or a lack of interest in performing the task. It seems that interest is an imperative. As Coyle describes it, "ignition" is an important factor for adaptive learning. Coyle's "ignition" must precede the myelin wrapping associated with practice. Much more than myelin theory is going on, which is beyond the scope of this book.

Conrad recently submitted a paper that was accepted after peer review. The paper was presented at the Institute of Industrial Engineers' (IIE's) annual Lean Six Sigma conference.[6] The applied research that he conducted sought to corroborate Mike Rother's experiences with adaptability within the manufacturing sector in a service-oriented environment. He compared Improvement Kata and Problem-Solving Kata cycling as an indicator of adaptability.

Results from the applied research are presented in Table 9.1. Adaptability is assumed to increase with faster cycling. The Improvement Kata is shown

Table 9.1 PDCA Cycle Rates for the PS and Improvement Kata

	PS Kata			*Improvement Kata*	
	Cycles	*Duration (d)*		*Cycles*	*Duration (d)*
Subject 1	1	27	Subject 7	4	6
Subject 2	1.5	22	Subject 8	15	35
Subject 3	0	8	Subject 9	7	19
Subject 4	1	11	Subject 10	6	12
Subject 5	1	12	Subject 11	7	11
Subject 6	1	13	Subject 12	5	13
Average	0.917	15.5	Average	7.3	16

to have cycled seven times faster than the Problem-Solving Kata in these experiments. Anecdotal evidence seemed to indicate that the Improvement Kata did indeed provide more satisfaction.

9.3 Conclusion

Adaptability became the factor that most piqued our interest in the *Toyota Kata* in the first place. We have enough field experience to appreciate that the most important aspect in implementing any Lean solution relies on the workforce's acceptance of it. Before endorsing the method in this book, we felt it necessary to convince ourselves of the kata efficacy, which precipitated our research efforts. Our results are the major reason that we are confident in recommending that the Improvement Kata be the first kata practiced. We now recognize the Improvement Kata as Lean's cultural modifier.

As Training Within Industry (TWI) trainers, we immediately recognized the connection between the Toyota Kata and TWI's application of PDCA as being nearly identical. We had experienced tepid results with TWI customers that did not immediately practice what they had learned in the courses. Our epiphany may seem obvious, but moving TWI from training only to training bolstered by skill acquisition gained through focused frequent practice is something that we knew had not been emphasized. Trumpeting the marriage between the Toyota Kata and TWI has become our calling.

Good luck!

Appendix: Lean Training Within Industry (TWI) Timeline

Timeline for Significant Items Related to Lean and TWI

445 BC: Sophocles is attributed to have talked about the concept of *learn by doing flow.*

215 BC: First assembly line production, Terra Cotta Warriors, near X'ian, Shaanxi province in China.

90 BC: Earliest treatise on mnemonics, *Rhetorica ad Herennium*, formerly attributed to Cicero.

1020: Ibn al-Haytham, the use of empiricism and learning through testing.

1466–1536: Best memory is based on understanding, system, and care; Desiderius Erasmus.

1525: First large-scale production-line building of warships at the Venetian Arsenal, supported partially later by Ferdinand I, grand duke of Tuscany of the Medici family.

1574: King Henry III of France visits Venice Arsenal, where building of galley ships using *continuous flow* processes happens in less than an hour.

1610: Galileo Galilei conducts designed experiments.
Francis Bacon, interplay between deductive and inductive reasoning.

1637: *Four Rules of the Cartesian Scientific Method,* by Rene Descartes.

1760: French General Jean-Baptiste Vaquette de Gribeauval grasped significance of *standardized* interchangeable parts for battlefield repair of artillery.

1776: *An Inquiry into the Nature and Causes of the Wealth of Nations,* by Adam Smith.

1781: Hydraulic spinning machine factory built by Richard Arkwright.

1785: William Playfair publishes first use of line charts and bar charts.

1799: Eli Whitney utilizes interchangeability of parts for contract of 10,000 muskets for the U.S. Army.

1802–1806: *Theory of Herbartianism* set out in advocating five formal steps in teaching by Johann Friedrich Herbart.

1807: Equipment devised to make simple wooden identical items in process sequence one at a time by Marc Brunel in England.

1822: Thomas Blanchard at Springfield Armory in the United States uses multiples sets of machines in *cellular arrangements* that could complete items with no human labor and in *single piece flow*.

1830–37: Eli Terry and Jerome Chauncy, first usage *of interchangeable* assembly with brass gears in clocks.

1832: *On the Economy of Machinery and Manufactures,* by Charles Babbage, the first work on operations research.

1867: *Das Kapital,* by Karl Marx.

1872: Metaphysical Club formed in Cambridge, Massachusetts, linked to the philosophy of Pragmatism.

1880: American Society of Mechanical Engineers is founded.

1882: Frederick W. Taylor begins time studies at Midvale Steel Company.

1885: Frank B. Gilbreth begins motions studies.

1890: Sakichi Toyoda invents a wooden handloom.

1892: Frank B. Gilbreth studies the motions of bricklayers.

1893: Frederick W. Taylor begins work as an engineer.

1894: First production automobile, the Victoria, by Karl Benz.

1896: *A Piece-Rate System*, by Frederick W. Taylor.

1900: "Ideal bureaucracy based on absolute authority, logic, and order," by Max Weber.

1901: National Bureau of Standards is established (precursor to National Institute of Standards and Technology).
First assembly line for automobiles in America, Ransom E. Olds.

1902: Sakichi Toyoda establishes concept of jidoka.

1903: Henry Ford produces the first Model A car.
Shop Management, by Frederick W. Taylor.

1906: Vilfredo Pareto creates mathematical formula to describe the 80–20 rule at the time describing wealth distribution.

1907: Frank B. Gilbreth applies time study in the construction industry.

1908: Henry Ford produces the Model T with interchangeable parts.

1910: Ford moves into Highland Park facilities.

1911: *The Principles of Scientific Management,* by Frederick Taylor.

1913: Henry Ford implements the moving assembly line.

1914: Clarence B. Thompson edits *Scientific Management,* a collection of Frederick W. Taylor's works.
The Psychology of Management, by Lillian Gilbreth.

1915: Frederick W. Taylor's system is in use at Niigata's Kamata plant in Japan.

1916: Council of National Defense established by the United States for the coordination of industries and resources for the national security and welfare.

1917: Henry L. Gantt develops the Gantt chart.
The Educative Process, by Chandler W. Bagley.
The Emergency Fleet Corporation is started with Charles R. Allen and Mike J. Kane employing Herbartianism-style training steps. Allen's now four-step method is used in 37 steel mills and 24 wood shipyards training 50,000 workers and later used as basis by M. Kane in TWI.

1919: *The Instructor, the Man, and the Job: A Handbook for Instructors of Industrial and Vocational Subjects,* by Charles R. Allen.
"How Training Departments Have Bettered Production," by U.S. Department of Labor Training Division, Training Bulletin #12, issued.

1920: *Mind and the World Order,* by Clarence Irving Lewis, which influences Walter A. Shewhart and Dr. W. Edwards Deming.

1921: Frank and Lillian Gilbreth introduce process analysis symbols to the American Society of Mechanical Engineers (ASME).

1922: *The Control of Quality in Manufacturing,* by George S. Radford.
Sakichi Toyoda invents the automatic loom.
The Foreman and His Job, by Charles Allen, "dealing with important factors in production; supervision, cost control and instruction."
Human Nature and Conduct, by John Dewey.

1924–1932: Famous Hawthorne Effect experiments take place at Western Electric factory outside Chicago (Skokie).
F. J. Roethlisberger and others employed by G. Elton Mayo to conduct Hawthorne studies.
Walter Shewhart starts study that will lead to the idea of control charts.

1925: Toshiro Ikeda translates Frederick W. Taylor's *Secrets of Eliminating Unprofitable Efforts* into Japanese.

1927–28: Henry Ford opens the Rouge Plant in Dearborn, Michigan. *Foremen's Lectures,* by Guy Via, quotes the four steps of Charles Allen: preparations, presentation, application, and testing.

1928: Chrysler starts DeSoto and Plymouth manufacture.

1929: Kiichiro Toyoda visits Ford's Rouge plant. Colorado State College uses Allen's four-step method in basic instructor courses. *The Quest for Certainty,* by John Dewey.

1930: Dr. W. A. Shewhart develops the statistical process control (SPC) chart. *Plant Training Practices,* by the American Telephone & Telegraph Company, with numerous discussions on industrial instruction.

1931: *Handbook of Business Administration,* edited by W. J. Donald, has numerous references to instruction steps.

1932: Taiichi Ohno joins Toyoda. American Society of Tool and Manufacturing Engineers (ASTME) is founded.

1933: *The Human Problems of an Industrialized Civilization,* by George Elton Mayo, lays groundwork for what later evolves into the Foundations for Good Relations. Automobile department established in Toyoda Auto Loom.

1936: Movie *Modern Times,* staring Charlie Chaplin.

1937: *Motion and Time Study,* by Ralph M. Barnes. Toyota Motor Company is founded, with Kiichiro Toyoda as president. J. M. Juran conceptualizes the Pareto principle to sort out the vital few from the trivial many. German aircraft industry pioneers takt time. Mitsubishi's technical relationship transfers this methodology to Japan, where, located nearby, Toyota learns and adopts it.

1938: Just-in-time concept established at Koromo/Honshoa plant by Kiichiro Toyoda.

1939: Dr. Walter A. Shewhart display's first version of the "Shewhart Cycle": specification, production, inspection. *Statistical Method from the Viewpoint of Quality Control* by Walter A. Shewhart, edited by 39-year-old W. Edwards Deming.

1940: Supply of steel and oil to Japan is cut off by U.S. President Roosevelt. U.S. Census Bureau states that more than eight million people are still unemployed, including three million who are involved in Works Progress Administration (WPA), Civilian Conservation Corps (CCC), and National Youth Association (NYA), W. Edwards Deming develops statistical sampling methods for the Census.

W. Edwards Deming teaches statistical process control techniques for wartime production.

Training Within Industry (TWI), one of the first emergency services, is organized "to utilize the talents of a voluntary staff."

F. J. Roethlisberger from Harvard University consults with TWI on Job Relations among other subjects.

Design of Job Instruction is started at lens grinding plant.

Job Instruction begins in England.

1941: Foundations for Good Relations solidified by TWI Service.

TWI Job Instruction Manual completed.

Job Relations and Job Methods under design assisted by F. J. Roethlisberger and John B. Fox of Harvard.

Management and Morale, by F. J. Roethlisberger.

1942: First design of Job Follow-Through (Coaching) is started.

National code entitled Basic Principles in Establishing Production Training in Shipyards, by TWI Service, endorsed and promoted by Maritime Commission.

1943: American Society of Mechanical Engineers (ASME) publishes standards and a glossary of terms.

Reader's Digest supplies 15,000 reprints of series of articles on TWI by Stuart Chase.

Job Relations article from *Reader's Digest* reprinted by the *Labor Messenger*, a newspaper affiliated with Houston Labor and Trades Council, and with the American Federation of Labor.

Coaching of Job Methods starts.

"Those Who Supervise Should Remember That All Workers Have Feelings," published in *Hospitals*, by Walter J. Dietz.

Taiichi Ohno transfers from Toyoda Auto Loom to Toyota Motor Corporation.

1944: Coaching for Job Relations starts.

TWI Job Instructions adapted and applied in nursing (health care).

"Learn to Work Well with Employees," published in *Modern Hospital*, by C. R. Dooley.

1945: *The Training Within Industry Report* is published by the U.S. government, stating that by this time more than 600 advisors and consultants had trained more than 23,000 prepared as TWI trainers (52% Job Instruction, 28% Job Relations, 20% Job Methods), who then trained almost two million certified supervisors in over 16,000 war production plants and essential services. In addition, more than 500,000 certifications had been provided to Army Service Forces, Civil Service Commission, U.S. Dept. of Agriculture, Social Security Board, Department of Labour Canada, and Ministry of Labour England.

TWI programs exported to Mexico, Saudi Arabia, South America, Australia, Holland, New Zealand, Poland, Norway, Sweden, Union of South Africa, Chile, Venezuela, Brazil, Cuba, India, Russia, Puerto Rico, and China.

TWI adapted for hospital, office work, libraries.

The TWI Field Services closed.

Shigeo Shingo presents "Production as a Network of Processes."

1946: American Society for Quality Control is founded.

TWI Foundation formed.

The Concept of the Corporation, by Peter Drucker.

Ford Corporation adopts General Motors' management style.

1947: Possibly first matrix management organization deployed at General Chemicals engineering department.

1948: *Methods Time Measurement,* by H. B. Maynard.

Larry D. Miles develops value analysis at General Electric.

Shigeo Shingo develops process-based machine layout.

Institute of Industrial Engineers (IIE) is founded.

Soichiro Honda founds Honda Motor Company.

1947–1949: Taiichi Ohno promoted to machine shop manager. Several concepts begin: elimination of waste, reduction of Work In Progress (WIP), in-process inspection, line stop authority to workers.

1950: Shigeo Shingo develops the single-minute exchange of dies (SMED).

Kaoru Ishikawa develops the cause-and-effect diagram with the addition of cards (CEDAC).

W. Edwards Deming modifies the Shewhart cycle at a Japanese Union of Scientists and Engineers (JUSE) meeting to *design, produce, sell, redesign* through marketing research.

1951: Lowell Mellen and associates from TWI Inc. teach more than 400 supervisors TWI in Japan under contract from the U.S. military; Mellen had been Cleveland TWI director.

W. Edwards Deming and Joseph M. Juran begin training the Japanese on quality control.

Taiichi Ohno learns and applies TWI in material shop at Koromo plant. He also becomes certified TWI trainer.

Deming Prize established.

Joseph M. Juran publishes *Quality Control Handbook* translated into Japanese.

Masaaki Imai publishes the recasting of the Deming wheel by JUSE to plan, do, check, action (PDCA).

1954: American Motors forms Hudson and Nash companies.
The Practice of Management, by Peter Drucker.

1955: Shigeo Shingo begins Toyota Motor Group lectures, "Separation of Workers and Machines."

1956: TWI Inc. provides Problem Solving in the Workplace training in Japan, employing PDCA framework.
Shigeo Shingo begins teaching P-Course on a regular basis at Toyota.

1957: Shigeo Shingo introduces the Scientific Thinking Mechanism for production improvements.

1958: *Hawthorne Revisited: Management and the Worker, Its Criticism, and Developments in Human Relations in Industry*, by Henry A. Landsberger.
Improving Managerial Performance, by Virgil K. Rowland, responsible for TWI implementation in the Hawaiian Islands, first successful user of Job Instruction in the office and helped develop Job Relations.

1959: *Landmarks of Tomorrow*, by Peter F. Drucker (knowledge worker).
Foremen in Action, by Glenn L. Gardiner, former TWI district director.

1960: *Managerial Performance Standards*, by Virgil K. Rowland.
Influencing Attitudes and Changing Behavior, by Zimbardo Ebbesen.
W. Edward Deming receives Japanese award Second Order of the Sacred Treasures.

1961: *Techniques of Value Analysis and Engineering*, by Lawrence D. Miles.
Shigeo Shingo devises the concepts of zero quality control, source inspection, and poka-yoke system.

1962: Quality circles begin at Toyota.
Makaaki Imai establishes the Kaizen Institute.

1965: Toyota wins the Deming Prize for Quality.
The Rational Manager, by Charles H. Kepner & Benjamin B. Tregoe.

1966: *Work and the Nature of Man*, by Frederick Herzberg.
Methods Engineering Designed Measurement Work Methods, by Edward V. Krick.

1968: F. J. Roethlisberger publishes *Man in Organization* essays.

1969: Toyota creates an Operations Management Consulting division.

1970: Walter Dietz publishes *Learn by Doing: The story of Training Within Industry,* citing, among other countries, the continuing use of TWI in England and New Zealand as of 1969.

1971: Taiichi Ohno completes the Toyota Production System.

1973: Worldwide oil shock plunges Japan economy into crisis; Toyota makes profit.

1974: Ford sees Mazda improving with kaizen.

1975: Shigeo Shingo extols the Nonstock Production System.

1976: *A New Approach to Production Systems through Developing Human Factors in Japan,* by R. Muramatsu and H. Miyazaka.

1977: Fallacies of MRP, by Nick Edwards, presented at APICS conference.

1978: *Complete Information of the Toyota Production System,* by Ikuro Takano.

1979: Ford buys 25 percent of Mazda to learn the Japanese manufacturing system firsthand.
Productivity Inc. formed by Norman Bodek.
"Quality Is Free: The Art of Making Quality Certain," by Phillip B. Crosby.

1980: *Study of the Toyota Production System from an Industrial Engineering Viewpoint,* by Shigeo Shingo.

1981: Shigeo Shingo's *Study of the Toyota Production System from and Industrial Engineering Viewpoint* is published in English.

1982: *Toyota's Strategy,* by F. Aona.
Genba Keiei published in English in 1988 as *Workplace Management,* by Taiichi Ohno.

1983: *Zero Inventories,* by Robert "Doc" Hall.

1984: *The Goal,* by Eliyahu M. Goldratt.
Management for Productivity, by John R. Schermerhorn, Jr.
Productivity Press formed by Norman Bodek.
Toyota/General Motors joint venture NUMII established in United States.

1985: *A Revolution in Manufacturing: The SMED System,* by Shigeo Shingo.
The Japanese Automobile Industry, Technology and Management at Nissan and Toyota, by Michael Cusumano.
Association for Manufacturing Excellence (AME) is formed.

1986: Deming reintroduces the Shewhart cycle as *plan, do, study, act.*
Kaizen: The Key to Japan's Competitive Success, by Masaaki Imai.

1988: Shingo Prize initiated at Utah State University by Norman Bodek and Professor Vern Buehler.

Toyota Production System: Beyond Large-Scale Production, by Taiichi Ohno and Norman Bodek.

Toyota manufacturing facility started in Georgetown, Kentucky.

Shingijutsu Co. Ltd. begins seminars and consulting in United States.

1991: *The Machine That Changed the World*, by James P. Womack.

Relevance Lost, by Tom Johnson and Robert Kaplan, on weaknesses in manufacturing accounting systems.

Continuous Improvement in Operations: A Systematic Approach to Waste Reduction, by Alan Robinson.

1992: *The Great Game of Business,* by Jack Stack and Bo Burlington.

1993: Mosaic is developed by Marc Andreesen, becoming the dominant navigation system for the World Wide Web.

1994: *The New Economics: For Industry, Government, Education*, by W. Edwards Deming.

1995: *Total Quality Management*, by Dale H. Besterfield.

1996: *Lean Thinking: Banish Waste and Create Wealth in Your Corporation,* by James P. Womack.

1997: *Becoming Lean: Inside Stories of U.S. Manufacturers*, by Jeffery K. Liker.

Gemba Kaizen, by Masaaki Imai.

1999: *Learning to See: Value Stream Mapping to Add Value and Eliminate MUDA*, by John Shook and Mike Rother.

Decoding the DNA of the Toyota Production System, by Steven J. Spear and H. Kent Bowen.

"The Toyota Production System: An Example of Managing Complex Social/Technical Systems. 5 Rules for Designing, Operating, and Improving Activities, Activity-Connections and Flow-Paths," dissertation by Steven J. Spears.

2000: The TWI Institute is created by Robert Wrona and Pat Graupp to bring back TWI training.

2001: Toyota publishes "The Toyota Way 2001" pamphlet for its worldwide organizations emphasizing their Respect for People principle.

2002: *Lean Six Sigma*, by Michael L. George.

2003: *The Toyota Way: 14 Management Principles from the World's Greatest Manufacturer*, by Jeffery K. Liker.

"Better Thinking, Better Results," by Bob Emiliani and others; detailed case study of The Wiremold Company.

2004: *Kaikaku,* by Norman Bodek.

2005: *Training Within Industry: The Foundation of Lean*, by Donald Dinero.

Inside the Mind of Toyota: Management Principles for Enduring Growth, by Satoshi Hino

Myelinations: An Overlooked Mechanism of Synaptic Plasticity?, by R. Douglas Field.

2006: Society of Manufacturing Engineers (SME) offers Lean certifications (bronze, silver, and gold) in collaboration with the Association for Manufacturing Excellence (AME) and the Shingo Prize.

The TWI Workbook: Essential Skills for Supervisors, by Patrick Graupp and Robert J. Wrona.

2007: *Toyota Culture: The Heart and Soul of the Toyota Way*, by Jeffery K. Liker and Michael Hoseus.

Made to Stick: Why Some Ideas Survive and Others Die, by Chip and Dan Heath.

2008: *Toyota Talent*, by Jeffery K. Liker and David Meier.

Outliers: The Story of Success, by Malcolm Gladwell.

White Matter Matters, by R. Douglas Fields.

2009: *Fundamental Principles of Lean Manufacturing*, by Shigeo Shingo and Jeffery K. Liker.

The Talent Code: Greatness Isn't Born. It's Grown, Here's How," by Daniel Coyle.

2010: *Toyota Kata: Managing People for Improvement, Adaptiveness and Superior Results*, by Mike Rother.

Implementing TWI: Creating and Managing a Skills-Based Culture, by Patrick Graupp and Robert J. Wrona.

Switch: How to Change Things When Change Is Hard, by Chip and Dan Heath.

Adapt: Why Success Always Starts with Failure, by Tim Harford.

2011: *The Toyota Way to Lean Leadership: Achieving and Sustaining Excellence Through Leadership Development*, by Jeffrey K. Liker and Gary L. Convis.

2012: *The Seven Kata: Toyota Kata, TWI, and Lean Training*, by Conrad Soltero and Patrice J. Boutier.

Getting to Standard Work in Healthcare: Using TWI to Create a Foundation for Quality Care, by Patrick Graupp and Martha Purrier.

Material researched for historical dates and publications of the above came from many sources; significant sources are listed below:

Evolution of the PDCA Cycle, Ronald Moen, Clifford Norman, http://pkpinc.com/files/NA01MoenNormanFullpapaer.pdf, API Publications.

Kaizen Event Implementation Manual, 5th edition, by Geoffery Mika, 2006, Society of Manufacturing Engineering.

Job Instruction: Sessions Outline and Reference Material, War Production Board, Bureau of Training, Training Within Industry Service, 1944 (Washington, D.C., U.S. Government Printing Office).

Learn by Doing, by Walter Dietz, 1971, self-published.

The Roots of Lean, by Jim Huntzinger, 2002, article printed by Association for Manufacturing Excellence.

The Training Within Industry Report 1940–1945: A Record of the Development of Management Techniques for Improvement of Supervision—Their Use and the Results, 1945, War Manpower Commission Bureau of Training, Training Within Industry Service (Washington, D.C., U.S. Government Printing Office).

Book listings available at Amazon.com.

Records from SME, November 2011, courtesy of Bryan Lund at http://chapters.sme.org/204/TWI_Materials/National_Archives_March_2006/TWINationalArchives.htm.

Records, November 2011, from http://chapters.sme.org/204/TWI_Materials/TWIPage.htm.

Records, November 2011, courtesy of Mark Warren, http://tesla2.com/TEWResearch.html.

Records from November 2011, www.superfactory.com/content/timeline.html.

References

Chapter 1

1. Liker, Jeffrey K., and Timothy N. Ogden, 2011, *Toyota under Fire: Lessons for Turning Crisis into Opportunity*, New York, McGraw Hill, p. 13.
2. Kato, Isao and Art Smalley, 2011, *Toyota Kaizen Methods: Six Steps to Improvement*. New York, Productivity Press, p. 69.
3. Pirastech, Reza (Russ) M., and Robert E. Fox, 2010, *Profitability with No Boundaries*, Milwaukee, Quality Press, p. 99.
4. TWI Institute, 2003, *Job Instruction Training Delivery Manual*, Liverpool, NY, CNYTDO, p. 8.
5. Rother, Mike, 2010, *Toyota Kata*, New York, McGraw Hill, p. 18.
6. TWI Institute, 2003, *Job Instruction Training Delivery Manual*, Liverpool, NY, CNYTDO.
7. Rother, Mike, 2010, *Toyota Kata*, New York, McGraw Hill, p. 18.
8. TWI Institute, 2003, *Job Relations Training Delivery Manual*, Liverpool, NY, CNYTDO.
9. Rother, Mike, 2010, *Toyota Kata*, New York, McGraw Hill, p. 194.
10. TWI Institute, 2002, *Job Methods Training Delivery Manual*, Liverpool, NY, CNYTDO, pp. 11–12.
11. TWI Institute, 2008, *Job Safety Training Delivery Manual*, Liverpool, NY, CNYTDO, pp. 7–9.
12. Rother, Mike, 2010, *Toyota Kata*, New York, McGraw Hill, p. 237.
13. Rosenbaum, Michael, 2004, *Kata and the Transmission of Knowledge in Traditional Martial Arts*, Boston, YMAA Publication Center, p. xvii.
14. Ibid.
15. Liker, Jeffrey K., and Gary L. Convis, 2012, *The Toyota Way to Lean Leadership*, New York, McGraw Hill, p. 51.
16. Dinero, Donald A., 2005, *Training Within Industry: The Foundation of Lean*, New York, Productivity Press, p. 31.
17. Moen, Ronald, and Clifford Norman, 2009, Evolution of the PDCA Cycle, API Publications, pp. 5–9. http://pkpinc.com/files/NA01MoenNormanFullpaper.pdf (accessed October 1, 2011).

18. Rother, Mike, 2010, *Toyota Kata*, New York, McGraw Hill, pp. 142–152.
19. Hall, Doug, seminar discussion, Nov. 26, 2009, at Eureka Ranch, Newtown, OH; also, Samuel Beckett, 1983, *Worstward Ho*, "*All of old. Nothing else ever. Ever tried. Ever failed. No matter. Try again. Fail again. Fail Better,*" New York, Grove Press; also in magazine *Fast Company*, Aug. 31, 1997, credit is given to David Kelly of Ideo to having said, "*Fail faster so they can succeed sooner*"; also, Tom Peters credits David Kelly of saying "*Fail. Forward. Fast. Fail faster, succeed faster*"; also, Alexander B. van Putten and Ian C. MacMillan, 2008, *Unlocking Opportunities for Growth: How to Profit from Uncertainty While Limiting Your Risk*, Pearson Prentice Hall, Upper Saddle River, New Jersey; also, Richard Farson, 2002, *Whoever Makes the Most Mistakes Wins: The Paradox of Innovation*, New York, The Free Press; also, Tom Kelley and Jonathan Littman, 2001, *The Art of Innovation: Lessons in Creativity from IDEO, America's Leading Design Firm*, New York, Doubleday.
20. Liker, Jeffrey K., 2004, *The Toyota Way: 14 Management Principles from the World's Greatest Manufacturer*, New York, McGraw Hill, pp. 52–58.
21. Liker, Jeffrey K., and James K. Franz, 2011, *The Toyota Way to Continuous Improvement*, New York, McGraw Hill, pp. 391–392.
22. Rother, Mike, 2010, *Toyota Kata*, New York, McGraw Hill, p. 186.
23. TWI Institute, 2003, *Job Instruction Training Delivery Manual*, Liverpool, NY, CNYTDO, p. 73.
24. War Manpower Commission, 1945, *The Training Within Industry Report, 1940–1945 A record of the Development of Management Techniques for Improvement of Supervision—Their Use and the Results*, Washington D.C., Bureau of Training, pp. 2–45.
25. Dietz, Walter, with Betty W. Bevens, 1970, *Learn by Doing: The Story of Training Within Industry 1940–1970*, Summit, New Jersey, self-published.
26. Weightman, Gavin, 2007, *The Industrial Revolutionaries: The Making of the Modern World, 1776–1994*, New York, Grove Press, pp. 285–292.
27. Ibid.
28. Ibid.
29. Womack, James, and Daniel T. Jones, 2005, *Lean Solutions*, New York, Free Press, pp. 35–39.
30. Rother, Mike, and John Shook, 1998, *Learning to See: Value Stream Mapping to Add Value and Eliminate Waste*, Brookline, MA, Lean Enterprise Institute, pp. 80–83.

Chapter 2

1. Liker, Jeffrey K., and Timothy N. Ogden, 2011, *Toyota under Fire: Lessons for Turning Crisis into Opportunity*, New York, McGraw Hill, pp. 8–9.
2. Rother, Mike, 2011, verbal discussion at Toyota Kata Floor Workshop Training, Ann Arbor, MI, University of Michigan.

3. Liker, Jeffrey K., and Ogden, Timothy N., 2011, *Toyota under Fire: Lessons for Turning Crisis into Opportunity*, New York, McGraw Hill, p. 13.

4. Rother, Mike, 2010, *Toyota Kata*, New York, McGraw Hill, p. 18.

5. Rother, Mike, 2011, verbal discussion at Toyota Kata Floor Workshop Training, Ann Arbor, MI, University of Michigan.

6. Rother, Mike, 2010, *Toyota Kata*, New York, McGraw Hill, pp. 266–274.

7. Rother, Mike, and John Shook, 1998, *Learning to See: Value Stream Mapping to Add Value and Eliminate Waste*, Brookline, MA, Lean Enterprise Institute.

8. Rother, Mike, 2011, *Improvement Kata Shop-Floor Handbook*, www-personal. umich.edu/~mrother/Homepage.html (accessed August 12, 2011).

9. Rother, Mike, 2011, verbal discussion at Toyota Kata Floor Workshop Training, Ann Arbor, MI, University of Michigan.

10. Osono, Emi, Norihiko Shimizu, et al., 2008, *Extreme Toyota: Radical Contradictions That Drive Success at the World's Best Manufacturer*, Hoboken, New Jersey, John Wiley & Sons, Inc. p. 146.

Chapter 3

1. TWI Institute, 2003, *Job Instruction Training Delivery Manual*, Liverpool, NY, CNYTDO, p. 16.

2. Coyle, Daniel, 2009, *The Talent Code: Greatness Isn't Born. It's Grown, Here's How*, New York, Bantam Books, pp. 64–65.

3. Seeley, Levi, 1899, *History of Education*, Ithaca, New York, Cornell University Library, p. 282.

4. War Manpower Commission, 1945, *The Training Within Industry Report, 1940–1945, A record of the Development of Management Techniques for Improvement of Supervision—Their Use and the Results*, Washington D.C., Bureau of Training, p. 45.

5. Graupp, Patrick, 2011, Personal correspondence and conversations.

6. Huntzinger, Jim, 2002, "The Roots of Lean," Association for Manufacturing Excellence, p. 8.

7. Ibid.

8. Allen, Charles R., 2010 reprint, *The Instructor; The Man and the Job: A Handbook for Instructors of Industrial and Vocational Subjects*, Memphis, TN, General Books, p. 73, Original 1919, J.B. Lippincott Company, Philadelphia and London, p. 129.

9. Huntzinger, Jim, 2002, "The Roots of Lean," Association for Manufacturing Excellence, p. 8.

10. Dennis, Pascal, 2002, *Lean Production Simplified: A Plain Language Guide to the World's Most Powerful Production System*, New York, Productivity Press, pp. 56; also, personal discussions with Patrick Graupp in 2011.

11. TWI Institute, 2003, *Job Instruction Training Delivery Manual*, Liverpool, NY, CNYTDO, p. 36.

12. Dietz, Walter, with Betty W. Bevens, 1970, *Learn by Doing: The Story of Training Within Industry 1940–1970*, Summit, New Jersey, self-published.
13. Wrona, Robert, 2004, *TWI: The Missing Link to Continuous Improvement*, presentation made available to TWI Trainers, TWI Institute, Syracuse, NY.
14. Rother, Mike, 2009, *Improvement Kata Shop-Floor Handbook, Teaching the Improvement Kata: Coaching Cycles*, p. 5, www-personal.umich. edu/~mrother/Homepage.html, (accessed August 12, 2011); also referenced in Mike Rother, 2009, *Toyota Kata*, New York, McGraw Hill.

Chapter 4

1. Liker, Jeffrey K., and Timothy N. Ogden, 2011, *Toyota under Fire: Lessons for Turning Crisis into Opportunity*, New York, McGraw Hill, pp. 27–28.
2. Webster's Online Dictionary, 2011, http://www.websters-online-dictionary. org/definitions/preceptor?cx=partner-pub-0939450753529744%3Av0qd01-tdlq&cof=FORID%3A9&ie=UTF-8&q=preceptor&sa=Search#922 (accessed November 14, 2011).
3. *Webster's Online Dictionary*, 2011, http://www.websters-online-dictionary. org/definitions/preceptor?cx=partner-pub-0939450753529744%Av0qd01-tdlq&cof=FORID%3A&ie=UTF-8&q=preceptors&sa=Search#922
4. Johann Friedrich Herbart (1776–1841), His theory of education—known as Herbartianism—was set out principally in two works, Pestalozzis Idee eines A B C der Anschauung (1802, *Pestalozzi's Idea of an A B C of Sense Perception*) and Allgemeine Pädagogik (1806, *Universal Pedagogy*), which advocated five formal steps in teaching.
5. TWI Institute, 2003, *Job Instruction Training Delivery Manual*, Liverpool, NY, CNYTDO.
6. Reynolds, Frank, 2005, "Coaching Philosophy," http://www.brianmac.co.uk/ coachphil.htm (accessed November 24, 2011).
7. Liker, Jeffrey K., 2003, *The Toyota Way, 14 Management Principles from the World's Greatest Manufacturer*, New York, McGraw Hill, p. 260.
8. Rother, Mike, 2011, verbal discussion at Toyota Kata Floor Workshop Training, Ann Arbor, MI, University of Michigan.
9. TWI Institute, 2003, *Job Instruction Training Delivery Manual*, Liverpool, NY, CNYTDO, p. 14.
10. Reynolds, Frank, 2005, "Coaching Philosophy," http://www.brianmac.co.uk/ coachphil.htm (accessed November 24, 2011).
11. Rother, Mike, 2011, *Improvement Kata Shop-Floor Handbook*, www-personal. umich.edu/~mrother/Homepage.html (accessed November 14, 2011).
12. Baddeley, Alan, 1997, *Human Memory: Theory and Practice*, East Sussex, UK, Psychology Press, Ltd., p. 110.
13. Rother, Mike, 2010, *Toyota Kata*, New York, McGraw Hill, pp. 257–258.

14. Liker, Jeffrey K. and Gary L. Convis, 2011, *The Toyota Way to Lean Leadership: Achieving and Sustaining Excellence Through Leadership Development,* New York, McGraw Hill, p. 13.
15. Rother, Mike, 2011, *Improvement Kata Shop-Floor Handbook,* www-personal. umich.edu/~mrother/Homepage.html (accessed November 14, 2011).
16. Rother, Mike, 2010, *Toyota Kata,* New York, McGraw Hill, p. 247.
17. Ibid, pp. 248–260.
18. Graupp, Patrick, and Robert Wrona, 2011, *Implementing TWI,* New York, Productivity Press, pp. 73–74.
19. Rother, Mike, 2011, verbal discussion at Toyota Kata Floor Workshop Training, Ann Arbor, MI, University of Michigan, relating specifically to the first-day seminar, section 7 slide 22.

Chapter 5

1. Shewhart, Walter A., 1939, *Statistical Method from the Viewpoint of Quality Control,* Graduate School of Department of Agriculture, Dover, re-issue by Dover, 1986, p. 45.
2. Dennis, Pascal, 2006, *Getting the Right Things Done: A Leader's Guide to Planning and Execution,* Cambridge, MA, p. 36.
3. Japan Human Relations Association, 1992, *Kaizen Tiean,* Portland, OR, Productivity Press, p. 45.
4. *"Problem well stated is half solved,"* Commonly attributed to Charles Kettering without sourcing: Charles Kettering, BrainyQuote.com, Xplore Inc, 2011. http://www.brainyquote.com/quotes/quotes/c/charlesket181210.html (accessed November 30, 2011).
5. Rother, Mike, 2011, *Improvement Kata Shop-Floor Handbook,* www-personal. umich.edu/~mrother/Homepage.html 4-PDCA.pdf (accessed November 2011), p. 14, ver. 8.
6. Liker, Jeffrey K., and Timothy N. Ogden, 2011, *Toyota under Fire: Lessons for Turning Crisis into Opportunity,* New York, McGraw Hill, p. 9.
7. Rother, Mike, 2011, *Improvement Kata Shop-Floor Handbook,* www-personal. umich.edu/~mrother/Homepage.html.
8. Dennis, Pascal, 2007, *Lean Production Simplified,* Boca Raton, FL, CRC Press, 2nd Edition, p. 107.
9. Dennis, Pascal, 2007, *Lean Production Simplified,* Boca Raton, FL, CRC Press, 2nd Edition, pp. 110–115.
10. Liker, Jeffrey K., and Timothy N. Ogden, 2011, *Toyota under Fire: Lessons for Turning Crisis into Opportunity,* New York, McGraw Hill, pp. 51–55.
11. TWI Institute, 2009, *Problem Solving Training Delivery Manual,* Liverpool, NY, CNYTDO.
12. Kato, Isao and Art Smalley, 2011, *Toyota Kaizen Methods: Six Steps to Improvement.* New York, Productivity Press, p. 69.

13. This statement is widely attributed to Albert Einstein, so for recognition purposes that's what is here. The research available tends to indicate that William Bruce Cameron, in a 1963 text "Informal Sociology: A Casual Introduction to Sociological Thinking," may have been the first recorded instance. Note that Albert Einstein's death was in 1955.

14. The practice of going slow to go fast can be traced to principle 13 of the *Toyota Way*, which states, "make decisions slowly by consensus, thoroughly considering all options; implement rapidly." See Liker, Jeffrey K., 2003, *The Toyota Way, 14 Management Principles from the World's Greatest Manufacturer*, New York, McGraw Hill, p. 237.

15. Osono, Emi, Norihiko Shimizu, et al., 2008, *Extreme Toyota: Radical Contradictions That Drive Success at the World's Best Manufacturer*, Hoboken, New Jersey, John Wiley & Sons, Inc. pp. 9–10.

Chapter 6

1. Shook, John J., 2011, "How to Go to the Gemba: Go See, Ask Why, Show Respect," June 21, http://www.lean.org/common/display/?o=1843.

2. TWI Institute, 2003, *Job Relations Training Delivery Manual*, Liverpool, NY, CNYTD.

Chapter 7

1. Mann, David, 2005, *Creating a Lean Culture: Tools to Sustain Lean Conversations*, Productivity Press, New York, pp. 25–37.

2. TWI Institute, 2008, *Job Safety Training Delivery Manual*, Liverpool, NY, CNYTDO.

3. U.S. Department of Labor, OHSA, 2011, Occupational Safety and Health Standards, H, Hazardous Materials, Compliance Guidelines, http://www.osha.gov/pls/oshaweb/owadisp.show_document?p_id=9768&p_table=STANDARDS, p. 1.

4. U.S. Department of Labor, OHSA, 2011, *Small Business Handbook*, 2209–02R 2005 http://www.osha.gov/Publications/smallbusiness/small-business.html.

5. TWI Institute, 2003, *Job Instruction Training Delivery Manual*, Liverpool, NY, CNYTDO, pp. 11,36,37,91.

6. Smalley, Art, 2006, *Summary Notes from Art Smalley Interview with Mr. Isao Kata*, ArtofLean.com.

7. Liker, Jeffrey K., and Timothy N. Ogden, 2011, *Toyota under Fire: Lessons for Turning Crisis into Opportunity*, New York, McGraw Hill, p. 8.

Chapter 8

1. Kipling, Rudyard, 1912, *Just So Stories*, "The Elephant's Child," London, Garden City Publishing.
2. Vlastos, Gregory, 1983, *The Socratic Elenchus, Oxford Studies in Ancient Philosophy I*, Oxford, Princeton University Press, Princeton, New Jersey, pp. 27–58.

Chapter 9

1. Covey, Stephen, 1989, *The Seven Habits of Highly Effective People, Restoring the Character Ethic*, New York, Free Press.
2. Commonly attributed quote to Bill Gates, with no definitive references.
3. Spear, Steven, and H. Kent Bowen, 1999, "Decoding the DNA of the Toyota Production System," Boston, *Harvard Business Review,* September–October. pp. 1–13.
4. Coyle, Daniel, 2009, *The Talent Code: Greatness Isn't Born. It's Grown, Here's How*, New York, Bantam Books, p. 6.
5. Ibid.
6. Soltero, Conrad, 2011, "Inculcating Adaptive Behavior Patterns in Complex Organizational Systems," IIE Engineering Lean and Six Sigma Conference, Atlanta, Sept. 12–14, conference proceedings, www.iienet.org/leansixsigma.

Biographies

Pat Boutier has more than 30 years of technical and business experience and assists companies to experiment and manage the implementation of radio frequency identification (RFID) solutions. He also works with companies in implementing, experimenting, and increasing their knowledge of Lean techniques, working with processes that cover a wide variety of equipment and services. He is a Shingo prize examiner, a Lean Six Sigma black belt, and is certified as a Training Within Industry (TWI) trainer in Job Relations, Job Methods, Job Instructions, Job Safety, and Problem Solving. His professional background includes gaining a wide range of expertise from engineering, production, purchasing, accounting, finance, mentoring, business tactics, and negotiations, allowing him to assist companies in holistic approaches to increasing their competitiveness.

He started his career working as an intern with the Chicago Transit Authority designing rail cars and then as a microwave design engineer at Motorola for more than 16 years, working in various engineering and manufacturing positions as engineering manager and production manager. As a vice president of operations for a contract manufacturing company, he turned a bankrupt operation into a profitable venture within one year. Later, he managed multiple plants at Tandy Electronics, directing their purchasing and manufacturing operations for computers. He then founded and managed his own company, designing and manufacturing vision systems for handicapped and municipal applications. In seven years at Texas Manufacturing Assistance Center (TMAC), he has assisted companies in coal mines, coal-fired and nuclear reactor power generation, liquid process, metal processing, food, chemical, cosmetic, furniture, sewing, electronic, defense, office, and hospital processes.

He has a BSEE in microwave quantum effects and feedback control from Marquette University and an MBA with marketing option from Loyola University. Along with being CompTIA RFID+ certified, he has also received his Bronze Certificate in Lean. He continues to expand his knowledge and involvement with many other certifications including ISO lead auditing and Toyota Kata.

His personal hobbies include league soccer, scuba diving, skiing, and reading. He is the proud father of daughter Danielle, who lives in California. He lives in Grapevine, Texas, and is blessed with a wonderful wife, Bernadette, and two younger children, Rachel and Andrew.

Conrad Soltero works at the University of Texas at El Paso for the Texas Manufacturing Assistance Center, a National Institute of Standards and Technology Manufacturing Extension Partnership (NIST MEP) affiliate. For the last 16 years, he has provided industry with a wide array of management and workforce development services. Areas of professional interest include systems engineering, economics, innovation, and policy analysis.

During his tenure in industrial extension, Conrad has provided technology transfer services for industries as diverse as automotive, electronics, plastics, primary metals, metal stamping, consumer products, printing, signage, packaging, apparel, food processing, cartridge remanufacture, medical garment convertor, medical device testing laboratory, employee leasing, executive search, manufacturing representation, document imaging, security equipment manufacture, government contracting, aerospace, financial services, software development, level one trauma center, and a publicly funded hospital.

Conrad is certified through the TWI Institute as a trainer in Job Instruction, Job Relations, Job Methods, Problem Solving, and Job Safety. He is a Six Sigma black belt and a Shingo research prize examiner. He has been published in various trade, environmental, and industrial engineering journals.

Conrad has completed BS and MS degrees in metallurgical and materials engineering. Aside from the vast array of industry sectors that he has worked with through industrial extension, his work background includes food service, automotive, and consumer products.

Conrad aspires to write a syndicated column on the politics of science and technology and maintains interests in travel, camping, jogging, hiking, cuisine, geography, and current events. He resides in El Paso, Texas, with his sweetheart of 30 years, Ms. Dana Gray, and their cat, Stalker.

Index

Page numbers followed by f indicate figure

Printed in the United States
by Baker & Taylor Publisher Services

Printed in the United States
by Baker & Taylor Publisher Services